SCRAPPY
CHURCH

Other Books by Thom S. Rainer

Becoming a Welcoming Church
We Want You Here
Who Moved My Pulpit?
I Will
Autopsy of a Deceased Church
I Am a Church Member
The Millennials*
Transformational Church*
Simple Life*
Essential Church*
Vibrant Church*
Raising Dad*
Simple Church*
The Unexpected Journey
Breakout Churches
The Unchurched Next Door
Surprising Insights from the Unchurched
Eating the Elephant (revised edition)*
High Expectations
The Every Church Guide to Growth+
The Bridger Generation
Effective Evangelistic Churches
The Church Growth Encyclopedia+
Experiencing Personal Revival*
Giant Awakenings
Biblical Standards for Evangelists*
Eating the Elephant
The Book of Church Growth
Evangelism in the Twenty-First Century+

*Coauthor
+Editor

SCRAPPY
CHURCH

GOD'S NOT DONE YET

Thom S. Rainer

PUBLISHING GROUP

NASHVILLE, TENNESSEE

978-1-5359-4581-3

Published by B&H Publishing Group
Nashville, Tennessee

Cover illustration by Mónica de Rivas.

Dewey Decimal Classification: 254
Subject Heading: CHURCH / CHURCH ADMINISTRATION /
CHURCH AND COMMUNITY

3 4 5 6 7 8 • 23 22 21 20 19

To

Ahkeem Abdul Morella
Your friendship defies description

———

And always to
Nellie Jo
My wife
My beach girl

Contents

Acknowledgments

THANK YOU. I CAN'T SAY IT ENOUGH. THANK YOU. FOR nearly thirty books, you readers have stayed with me. You have engaged with me. You have encouraged me. You have blessed me. I don't take you for granted. And I pray God will continue to use my books for His glory in His churches.

The great challenge of an acknowledgment section is giving credit where credit is due. And to be sure, I am part of a large team of family, friends, and coworkers. They all deserve so much more credit than I give them.

Thank you, B&H team. You are the best. You are the best Christian publisher around. I am honored to serve with you. Thank you to all the B&H team, with a specific word of gratitude to Jennifer Lyell and her leadership. Jennifer and I have worked at two organizations together. I count it all joy. Thank you also to Devin Maddox, my editor cum laude.

You probably have heard me mention Team Rainer. Many of you have come to know them from the podcasts and the ThomRainer.com blog. You remember their names: Amy

Jordan, Amy Thompson, Jonathan Howe, Jana Biesecker, Julie Masson, and Bryan Underwood. I am blessed beyond measure to serve alongside these men and women.

I am likewise blessed to be a part of the ministry of LifeWay Christian Resources and our five thousand employees. Specifically, I give thanks for the leadership and friendship of LifeWay's executive leadership team: Brad Waggoner, Selma Wilson, Earl Roberson, Connia Nelson, Tim Hill, and Joe Walker. You are great leaders. You are great friends.

I have been told our community, those who connect with my blogs, podcast, books, and Church Answers each year, is around fourteen million people. That blows my mind. I am so grateful for all of you. You bless me by connecting with me through my books, my blog, ThomRainer.com, my podcasts, *Rainer on Leadership* and *Revitalize and Replant*, and my sub-scription ministry, Church Answers. You have come to learn from me, but I have learned so much more from you.

I love my family. I really do love my family. A follower on Twitter recently told me my love for my family was the most obvious thing about me. I consider those words some of the greatest encouragement I have ever received.

You know the name and beauty of Nellie Jo, my bride for forty-one years. And you know how I thank God for my three sons and their wives: Sam and Erin, Art and Sarah, and Jess and Rachel. But you also know how blessed I am with the ten Rainer grandchildren they have given Nellie Jo and me: Canon,

Maggie, Nathaniel, Will, Harper, Bren, Joshua, Collins, Joel, and James.

This book is a composite of conversations, interviews, and comments from an amalgamation of church leaders. The names have been changed and some of the details are different to protect anonymity where it was necessary. Some of the stories are individual stories; some are composite stories. But for all those who spoke with me, shared with me, laughed with me, and, on occasion, cried with me—thank you. This book is your story. And your story will have a profound impact on many.

You are part of the scrappy church revolution. It is a powerful story that is just beginning to unfold. Wait for it. Watch for it. And become a part of it.

See the great things our God will do.

CHAPTER 1

Why You Should Have Hope for Your Church

AMAZON.

The name evokes the spectrum of emotions.

For some, the name means an incredible selection of resources, unparalleled delivery, amazing customer service, and convenience not known just a decade or so ago. Amazon is what's right with the world. It's the embodiment of the future and the hope for society. If we are truly living in a material world, Amazon is king, queen, and crown prince of this world.

For others, the name evokes fear, distrust, and a disquieting sense of unfairness. You loathe Amazon, particularly if you make the fatal mistake to compete with the beast. The creature devours mom-and-pop stores. It disrupts industry after industry. It has the unfair advantage of hordes of cash and the favored status of countless government entities.

If you are in the former category, you shout exclamations of joy every time the box with the smile arrives at your porch. You celebrate one less trip and futile shopping effort to the mall. You express glee when your shipping charge is zero. Nothing. Nada. After all, you are part of the elect; you have Amazon Prime™.

But if you are in the latter category, you tremble with fear with each new Amazon pronouncement. They are the modern-era Langoliers, but they consume businesses instead of time. They are relentless, uncaring, and unforgiving. If you get in their way, you will be consumed. If you are fortunate, they will purchase you at a deep market value discount. Either way, you will cease to exist.

I admit my own schizophrenia with Amazon. I have been a customer of Amazon so long, I actually received a *handwritten* thank you note for being such a good customer many years ago. I was a Prime member before Prime membership was cool. And, as a confessing introvert, I absolutely love shopping without people around. As a consumer, I really do like Amazon.

But I have been on the other side of Amazon. They have been my competitor. The company I have led is not that small. We have a half-billion dollars in annual revenue and 5,000 employees. But we are gnats compared to the giant. In fact, I seriously doubt Jeff Bezos knows my name or my company. I have had to lead my organization to confront the stark realities of the massive Amazon. I know the challenges. I know the angst.

Hope in the Amazon World

We all know at least parts of the story of Amazon. Jeff Bezos started the company on July 5, 1994. One day after Independence Day, he began the organization upon which many of us would pledge our dependence. At its onset, Amazon was an online bookstore. Storing books in a garage, Bezos saved us a trip to the local bookstore. In the past quarter century, Amazon has entered so many industries and offered so many services, we've lost count of them. And in an amazing turn of events, Amazon has become the largest provider of cloud computing services in the world.

But Amazon started as an Internet bookstore. Amazon started in Bezos's garage. So, if any industry should be afraid of Amazon, it should be the book retailers, right? For certain, many of the big chains have felt the wrath of the Amazon power. Try to find a Borders bookstore in your town, and you will understand.

But something amazing has taken place in the shadow of the seemingly omnipotent Amazon: *Independent bookstores are not only surviving, many are thriving.*

This reality has flown under the radar of most observers. I guess most of us assumed the "indie" stores were long gone. Not so. To the contrary, it is a thriving industry. Dozens of articles are now surfacing about this resurgent and resilient business.

So what did the indies do?

They did not try to compete directly with Amazon. They did not offer Prime™. They did not sell a gadzillion books. They did not offer free shipping. And they did not offer endless streaming videos for you and your family to consume.

But they did connect with their communities. They did have fun events that reflected the hopes and dreams of those who lived nearby. They offered intensely personal services, not innately digital services. They curated their books so the consumer could better understand what was available. And they responded with new local ideas instead of new data-driven algorithms.

I know. This book is about churches, not Amazon. It's about reaching our community, not selling our books.

But I'm guessing you are understanding the reason for this early excursion. I think you get why I am writing about independent bookstores in a book about churches.

The main reason is to provide hope. And a close corollary is to demonstrate how that hope is actually played out in local congregations just like yours.

The Hope around Us

How many times have I heard such statements?

"We can't compete with the megachurch in our town!"

"A new church was started two blocks from us. We've got plenty of churches without them!"

"The church brought another one of their campuses near us. It's totally unethical what they are doing."

"We can't reach young families. They all go to the big church that has all the children's and student stuff."

"We don't have the money or the people the other churches have."

To answer my own question, I have heard comments like those hundreds, if not thousands, of times. They are statements of hopelessness. They are statements of despair. They are statements of defeat. They are statements of fear.

And to be fair, I get it. Those are not delusional statements. They are statements based upon the real and painful experiences of countless church members and church leaders. These church leaders don't want to feel this way. They desire to break out of the mediocrity of the same, lame, and tame existence of their churches. They want to make a difference. They want their churches to make a difference.

They want to know if there is hope. God's hope. God's possibilities.

And the answer is an unequivocal "yes!"

I do not make such a bold statement without basis. First, and above all, God is not done with your church. He put your church in your location for a reason. Do you really think He does not desire your church to become a potent force for Him in your community?

Second, I make the statement based upon the stories of other churches. I have seen too many so-called hopeless churches become turnaround churches. I have seen congregations defy all the doom-and-gloom prognosticators. I have seen churches spit in the face of the objective facts that say it can't be done.

I call these turnaround churches "scrappy churches."

Scrappy Churches and the Football Team

I like the word *scrappy*. It brings back memories of my high school football team. Yes, I know. I'm taking a trip to antiquity. But the memories of Johnny are vivid even today.

Johnny was our quarterback. He really got the position by default. We had no one who could throw the ball within ten yards of the intended receiver except Johnny. But we didn't have a lot of confidence in him as we began to go through the grueling two-a-day practices in the sweltering summer heat.

Johnny had never played quarterback. We won two out of ten games the previous year. The local pundits were wagering (yes, they really had a betting pool) we wouldn't win a game. After all, we were a lousy team the previous year without a proven quarterback. Why should anyone give us a chance this year?

But Johnny was scrappy. He worked relentlessly. He memorized the playbook for the quarterback. It was the most difficult playbook on the team. He ran hard. He exercised hard. He was determined he would not be defeated for lack of effort.

The rest of us on the team were inspired by Johnny. We became scrappy players just like him. We had an offensive lineman who weighed 160 pounds, but he was unbelievable with his blocking skills. He went against guys who weighed 70 pounds more than he did, and he took them to task.

One of our linebackers, weighing a similar 160 pounds, was a machine at tackling. He would not be deterred.

What about me? I know you are dying to ask. I was the tailback on the team, which meant I accounted for about 90 percent of the running plays. You can stop snickering now. It's true. The previous year I had been moved from linebacker to running back because I intercepted a pass and ran it for a touch-down. The coach thought if I could run that fast, I should be a running back.

So, I went from a total beginner to finishing fourth in the state in rushing and making the honorable mention all-state team. I even had a couple of scholarship offers at small colleges.

We became a scrappy team because we had a scrappy leader.

The other teams were bigger.

The other teams were faster.

The other teams were more athletic.

But we beat most of the other teams. We made it to the quarterfinals of the state playoffs.

We were scrappy. Johnny showed us how to be scrappy.

Undoubtedly, whether you're a Boomer, Gen Xer, or Millennial, you've seen the legendary 1993 film *Rudy*. Based on a true story, Rudy Ruettiger was a dyslexic, underweight boy who belonged to a family of Notre Dame football fanatics. In the Ruettiger household, there was no higher allegiance than to the Fighting Irish. After high school graduation, because of low grades—surely due in no small part to his dyslexia—Rudy's application to the University of Notre Dame was denied.

But even if he had been accepted, what were the chances a 5'6" 160-lb. kid from Joliet, Illinois, was going to play football for the mighty Irish anyway? The deck was stacked against him.

Rudy did not give up. He ignored convention. Rudy attended nearby community college Holy Cross and was accepted at Notre Dame two years later. Not only that, and you know how the story goes by now, Rudy's scrappiness off the field translated onto the field, and Rudy suited up for his childhood dream as a walk-on.

So, you are undoubtedly asking, what does a scrappy church really look like? Let's take a look.

Scrappy Church: God's Power at Work

Scrappy.
Feisty.
Tenacious.
Determined.

Dogged.

Persistent.

You get the picture.

These churches have leaders and members who refuse to give up. To the contrary, they have people in the congregation who truly believe the best days of the church are in the very near future. Sure, they have their frustrations. But they see the power of God working every week in their church. They are excited about both the present and the future. They don't see limitations; they see God's possibilities.

Kent is a pastor in upstate New York. He was warned by many people not to consider going to the church seven years ago. But he decided to listen to God rather than the naysayers. You see, Kent talked with several of the members as he was considering his call to pastor the church. His words are memorable, if not powerful.

"The church was in a tailspin," he began. "In its so-called glory days, the attendance almost reached 300. When I began talking to the church, it was closer to 100."

Then Kent began talking to some of the leaders. He was amazed. Totally amazed.

Beth had been at the church for more than forty years. "She began to share the opportunities to connect in the community. She knew everyone, and she had a plan for how the church could minister to them," Kent said. "Her vision was powerful and compelling."

He had another incredible conversation with Milt. He had been at the church for less than three years, but Milt too was excited about the possibilities. "Milt really understood the neighborhood around the church," Kent told us. "He may not be an expert in demographics, but he has an intuitive sense about the immediate area. I could really see God working in his ideas."

"Okay, Kent," we asked, "were there any pessimists in the bunch? After all, the church had declined by nearly 70 percent. Were all the conversations so rosy?"

Kent chuckled, "Of course not. There were a lot of defeated people in the church. There were some who told me outright that the church probably would not survive. Yeah, the hopeful ones were in the minority, but they were a God-powered minority!"

A God-powered minority. You've got to love it.

I guess you might expect to hear about the immediate turnaround of this church. Well . . . not exactly. Listen to Kent tell the story:

> "The first three years were pretty tough," he said frankly. "I have a lot of emotional scars from those early days. But God would not let the vision we had die. By year four we began to see some real turnaround. Now in my eighth year, we are truly a force for the kingdom in our community. We are almost as big as

the church was in the glory days, approaching three hundred in attendance. But our turnaround is more than numbers. It's much more than numbers."

We could park on Kent's story the rest of this book, but we have a bigger purpose. We want you to hear from hundreds of scrappy churches. We want you to see what God is doing in places where most have given up. We want you to hear the collective story instead of an isolated piece of hope here and there.

Before we go further, let's look at the "before and after" of the scrappy churches. Let's see six of the incredible transitions they made, transitions that defied the conventional wisdom that said it couldn't be done.

Transition 1: Excuses to Ownership

Fred serves a church near the Metroplex of Dallas. There is no shortage of people in the area. But Fred admits he started his leadership at the church with a ton of excuses.

"I didn't realize how excuse-driven I was," Fred told us. "For a few months I was pretty pumped about my leadership opportunity. The church was landlocked in an older neighborhood, and it had declined from around 275 in attendance to 130 the past ten years. I guess I thought I could just go in and lead a turnaround. I had never served as the lead pastor of a church, always in another staff position. And I was arrogant enough to believe I could do things so much better than the pastors I served under and all the pastors who preceded me at my church."

He paused. "But I was wrong," Fred admitted. "Dead wrong."

The church had a minor spike in attendance for about six months, then it resumed its pattern of decline.

So how did Fred respond?

"Excuses," he said flatly. "A bunch of excuses."

He began to reflect on the excuses. "I couldn't compete with the larger churches. That was my first excuse. Sure, they had more programs to offer than we did. I heard that specifically from members who left. They went where the action was."

He continued, "My next excuse was my neighborhood. It was transitioning in two ways. First, it had mostly transitioned to families with a lower income than the members of the church. Almost all those who attended were driving several miles to get to church. Second, some of the homes were being sold to higher-income families who were remodeling them. I would learn later the name of that transition was gentrification."

So Fred's church had seen lower-income residents move into the neighborhood for several years. Then a new trend developed where higher-end residents were populating the area.

"That's right," he affirmed. "I had excuses both ways. We couldn't reach the lower-income residents at first, then we couldn't reach the higher-income residents. I was making myself the victim of the Goldilocks syndrome. We had no chance unless the income of the residents was 'just right.'"

The church is now on a healthy path. Yes, the congregation still has challenges, but the trajectory is really encouraging. We asked Fred what precipitated the turnaround.

"God just woke me up," he responded. "In my prayer time, I began to realize I was leaning on excuses instead of leaning on God. He put my church at this address for a reason. He put me here for a reason. I decided to take responsibility for the leadership God gave me. I decided to move beyond excuses. My new attitude was the beginning of the turnaround."

Indeed. That was the beginning of the turnaround.

Transition 2: Obstacles to Allies

Leading a church would be a lot easier if we didn't have to deal with people.

The sentence is cliché, but it's true. Dealing with people is a messy business.

Not only do we have to deal with people in churches, we have to lead them *and* love them. It's the loving them part that can be really difficult.

Church members can be critics. Church members can be bullies. Church members can be undependable. Church members can be fickle.

To be fair, those church members are more the exception than the rule; but it doesn't take too many difficult church members to make our ministry really messy. The apostle Paul told us how to respond to difficult church members as he was dealing with the members at the church at Corinth. Right after he gave us a beautiful metaphor of members of the church being like members of the body (1 Cor. 12), he wrote these words to remind us about how we should treat each other:

> Love is patient, love is kind. Love does not envy, is not boastful, is not arrogant, is not rude, is not self-seeking, is not irritable, and does not keep a record of wrongs. (1 Cor. 13:4–5)

Do you get that? We are to love the members of the church without condition. They are not our obstacles. They should be our allies.

Patrick serves as a pastor in Oklahoma. It took him a while to understand that God gave us the members in our churches for a reason. They are members of the body of Christ. They are to be our allies, and we are to love them.

"When I realized God gave our church the members we had for a reason," he said, "it changed my perspective. I started asking them to tell me their stories. I asked them about their dreams for the church. I would then ask them how we could work together to reach God-given dreams for our church."

Patrick stared ahead for a moment in deep thought. He continued, "That was the key to our transition, I believe. God gave me a new heart for our members. They were no longer my obstacles. They were a part of the dream for the church. Our church really began to dream again."

Transition 3: Limitations to Abundance

Your church has everything it needs. Really. Let me put it another way. God has given your church all the resources you need to move forward.

You have enough money.

You have enough people.

You have adequate facilities.

You have enough people to reach.

You have the right aged people in your church.

It does you absolutely no good to complain that you don't have sufficient resources. It does you no good to imagine how much easier or better your church would be if you just had something else. A mind-set of limitations creates a limitation on your leadership.

You know this verse, don't you? "And my God will supply all your needs according to his riches in glory in Christ Jesus" (Phil. 4:19). Of course you do. But do you believe it for the church you lead? Do you think the Bible is applicable to other churches and leaders, but not your church and your leadership?

Your church has everything God says you need to move forward. You have everything you need to lead forward. Be a leader who truly believes in God's abundance rather than your perceived limitations.

Transition 4: Despair to Joy

"I entered vocational ministry with some naiveté," Marcus told us, "but I had a lot of joy. I was really excited about serving God's church. I don't know exactly when I started surrendering my joy to life's circumstances, but I know it happened. I let the underbelly of church life bring me down. I focused on the negatives more often than not. My whole perspective and attitude stunk!"

Marcus remembers specifically his shift in attitude. He was studying the book of Philippians and read these words in Philippians 4:4, 8: "Rejoice in the Lord always. I will say it again: Rejoice! . . . Finally brothers and sisters, whatever is true, whatever is just, whatever is lovely, whatever is commendable—if there is any moral excellence and if there is anything praiseworthy—dwell on these things."

"It hit me like a ton of bricks," Marcus exclaimed. "I was dwelling on the wrong things. I was focusing on the negatives rather than what God wants me to dwell on. That was a major attitude shift for me. It was amazing to watch the church follow my lead with a similar joyful attitude."

We heard statements like Marcus's again and again: "That was a major attitude shift for me." It seems like many of the scrappy churches had leaders who decided they would be scrappy in God's power.

Transition 5: Fear to Courage

"My name is Roger, and I was a coward." Roger smiled as he recited those words to us. He was remembering how he had become frozen with fear as pastor of the church. The scenario occurred four years earlier as Roger celebrated his fifty-fifth birthday.

"No, I didn't celebrate my birthday at all," he confessed. "I had heard from too many of my peers that another church would never consider me after I turned fifty-five. I felt stuck. Even worse, I began to live in fear."

Roger was in his second year at the church when he turned fifty-five. The church was in a slight but almost imperceptible decline. The members were mostly happy. And that became his de facto strategy: keep the members mostly happy and don't rock the boat.

The church continued its slow decline under his leadership, or perhaps more accurately, lack of leadership. He realized there was no such thing as status quo though. The church had to let go of a long-time staff member because the budget could no longer support him. Roger retreated into a greater depth of fear.

When we spoke to Roger, however, the church was on a healthy trajectory. It had turned a corner. Roger was leading from God-given confidence instead of human-centered fear. What, we asked, was the turning point?

His answer was a simple one-syllable word: "Peg."

Peg is Roger's wife. Seeing the misery evident in her husband's life and ministry, she confronted him.

"Peg held back no punches," Roger recalled. "She told me she would rather us lose our job than lose our vision. And she read the Bible to me. I remember the words of Joshua 1:9 even now: 'Haven't I commanded you: be strong and courageous? Do not be afraid or discouraged, for the LORD your God is with you wherever you go.'"

Roger paused, then resumed. "Peg told me I was living in fear and disobeying God because I was not trusting God. I was more concerned about a paycheck than obedience. My security was my job but not my God."

He smiled again. "I love that girl," he said. "She was so right. It was almost immediate for me. I began to lead again from a posture of faith and courage instead of fear. I will turn sixty on my next birthday, and I am more excited than ever to see what God will do next."

Transition 6: Impossible to Possible

"I am able to do all things through him who strengthens me" (Phil. 4:13).

My original title for this book was *The Impossible Turnaround Church*. I really liked conveying the idea that many churches were doing incredibly well despite the human odds that seemed stacked against them. But my publisher did not like the title. She said it was too general and could be taken in too many different ways.

She was right. We settled on *Scrappy Church* since it conveys the personalities of these turnaround churches.

But I still like the idea of how these churches demonstrated God's possibilities when most people would have deemed it impossible. I like how these leaders made profound decisions to change their own leadership approach to one of trust and excitement. I like how these churches did not accept the verdict of inevitability regarding their decline and demise. I like how these smaller and mid-sized churches survived and thrived, often in the shadows of larger churches.

They moved from the impossible to the possible.

Better stated, they moved from human impossibility to God's possibility.

So how did they do they it? What changed about them? What makes them different from other churches that have not seen a turnaround?

What did they do to prepare themselves to be a scrappy church?

Those are all excellent questions.

I will begin to answer them in the next chapter.

CHAPTER 2

Preparing to Be a Scrappy Church

IT WAS THE SUMMER OF 1940.

Hitler was leading the Nazi onslaught of Europe. Nation after nation was falling as the western march continued. France was defeated. Britain would certainly be next.

Winston Churchill had just become Prime Minister of Britain. The sentiment among the leaders of Britain to attempt to negotiate peace with Hitler was gaining favor with the War Cabinet, Parliament, and, at least initially, King George VI. The tide of civilization was about to turn.

Churchill indeed thought about negotiating a peace with Hitler. But as he mulled it over through sleepless nights, he saw the futility of negotiating with an evil tyrant. Such a move was tantamount to surrender. If Britain were to lose the war, it would be on their terms, fighting to the last.

He would not surrender.

Churchill passionately pleaded with Parliament and, through his speech, all the people of Britain. The nation followed his leadership. Against all seeming odds, Britain decided to fight Germany. And though it would be five years before Hitler and his forces were defeated, the tide turned on the day one man convinced others not to give up. Never. Never. Never give up.

The course of history changed. Civilization took a new course.

Never give up.

Never. Never. Never.

The Tenacious Scrappy Church

Comparisons, of course, are not perfect. The challenges of World War II and the plight of many churches are vastly different. I get that.

But there are many church leaders and church members today wondering if their churches will survive. They are discouraged. A number of them are defeated. For countless numbers, the best days seem to be in the past.

Those attitudes of pessimism and even defeat are not unwarranted. At least two-thirds of churches are declining, maybe more. We estimate that about 100 to 150 churches are closing every week. The sighs of despair are justified.

Even among those churches that are hanging on, a number of their leaders feel a sense of futility. Though smaller churches vastly outnumber larger churches, more people are attending the larger churches every week.[1] The migration from smaller to larger is clear and evident.

Church leaders and church members sense the shadow of the larger churches over them. They see their young families move to the churches that have ministries and programs for their children and teenagers. They see the newer, even cooler, buildings of the larger churches.

They see it. They sense it.

They know it.

Is there hope? Do these smaller churches have any path forward? Can the smaller and mid-sized church survive in the world seemingly dominated by larger churches and megachurches?

The answer to the question is an absolute "yes." I make that declaration not by sentiment nor false hopes, but by clear evidence of God's work. Though the number of scrappy churches is still relatively small, they are growing in number. I am convinced scrappy churches are a growing trend of the reality we will soon see.

So what are some of the characteristics we can already see in these scrappy churches? Let's look at a few.

They Believe God Still Has a Plan for Them

While scrappy church leaders are not blind to the difficulties around them and in their congregations, they remain certain God is still working in their churches. "We are at this address right now for a reason," one pastor told us. "We are not here by accident. We are determined to make a difference in our community. We are moving forward."

So does the church have challenges as they seek to move forward? The pastor responded with a loud laugh. "Of course we do. We have many of the same issues in our turnaround as we had in our decline. We still struggle for resources. We still have change-resistant members. We still have a lot of critics."

He paused for a moment and reflected, "But, you know, many of us in the church have chosen to focus on what God wants us to do. We have to be obedient to the Great Commission and the Great Commandment. We can't spend our time focusing on the critics and the naysayers. We have to focus on God's plan for us."

His concluding words were a common sentiment among the scrappy churches. "We believe with all our hearts that God still has a plan for our church."

It is that dogged determination in God's plan for the church that fuels them forward. They see their mission as God's mission and, because it is truly His, they will not be deterred.

They Turn to Prayer for the Turnaround

One of the common themes of the scrappy churches was a greater dependence on prayer for their churches. "We realized we had become comfortable in our own power," said Margaret, a member of one of the scrappy churches that experienced a turnaround. "We began a time of intensive prayer for our church. It began with a twenty-four-hour prayer vigil, but it continued well beyond that. In fact, we are still praying for God to use our church in the community and beyond. It's amazing what happens when you depend on Him through prayer."

Of course, it would be good if we could share with you exactly how these churches are moving forward in prayer. There is, however, no discernible pattern. The ways the churches have become focused on prayer for revitalization are as diverse as the churches themselves.

Though the methodologies are different, there is a theme of prayer in many of the scrappy churches. A number of the congregations focused on the role prayer played in the early church. In fact, this passage from Acts 2:42 is cited frequently in the scrappy churches: "They devoted themselves to the apostles' teaching, to the fellowship, to the breaking of bread, and to prayer."

Prayer is not an afterthought in scrappy churches. It is pervasive and powerful.

They Celebrate the Presence of Other Churches

"I used to get so angry every time a new church or new campus of a church located near us," Harold admitted. Harold is a pastor of a turnaround church. "I would fuss to whomever would listen. We don't need another church in this area!"

We also asked Harold what changed his attitude on this issue. He smiled, "My son. James is a pastor in Arizona. We stay in touch a lot. He heard my rants about the other churches for years. One Christmas, he and his family spent a week with us. He showed me the demographics near our church. And he showed about how much of our community is in church."

What did the report show?

Harold sighed, "More than 80 percent of our community is not in church. Probably almost as many aren't believers. James didn't have to say another word. I felt ashamed. We don't have too many churches. We don't have enough churches reaching people. I let anger and jealousy rule me. And it affected my leadership of the church."

What happened next?

"I wish I could say that I had a dramatic change," Harold began. "But over time, God began to work on me about this issue. My hard heart began to melt. I now see other churches as our allies in the mission of the kingdom. They are not our competition. I really think my change of heart was key to our church turning around eventually."

Harold's story is common in scrappy churches. We will expand on this issue toward the end of this chapter.

They Greatly Increase Their Efforts on Outward Focus

Here is a huge discovery we saw in the scrappy churches: They began to devote enormous resources to the Great Commission and the Great Commandment. Joey's story is emblematic of this change.

"I guess we were a typical church," Joey began. "By typical, I mean we were in slow decline. Most of our time and budget went to take care of our own needs. And our outreach was limited to one of two big emphases a year. We had a community fair in the spring and a big Christmas production for the community in December. But the rest of the year we really didn't do anything except for ourselves. We saw outreach as a seasonal event rather than an ongoing mind-set."

So what changed?

"Reality changed," Joey said. "Our slow decline meant we couldn't keep all of our staff. It eventually meant we couldn't keep up our facility. All of that was a wake-up call for us. He paused. "I wish I could say we had this great revival and God moved us to obedience," he continued. "But that's not what happened. We saw that the church we were trying to hold on to would disappear. Sadly, that was our wake-up call."

Joey's energy level increased visibly as he continued his story. "But, you know, God took our desperation and used it for His glory. We started more and more outreach to try to save our church, but God used it to begin to reach our community," he exclaimed. "The more we devoted our time and money to reach others," he continued, "the more we saw our impact on the community."

The church is now a vibrant congregation serving its community. "I look back over the past four years or so," Joey told us, "and I can't believe how many resources we are devoting to reaching and serving our community. It's probably four or five times greater."

Indeed, that multiplication of resources toward an outward focus was a common theme we heard from the scrappy churches. Incremental change didn't get it. It had to be radical change.

And that radical change led to a renewed congregation multiplying its resources to reach its community.

Blueprint for Preparation

On the one hand, I wish I could provide a detailed action plan to help churches move toward becoming a scrappy church. On the other hand, such a formulaic approach would suggest that all churches are alike. I love the diversity of churches across the globe and would never want to suggest they are monolithic.

But we do have a lot of information on scrappy churches. In fact, we have enough information to discern a blueprint for leaders to prepare to move in that direction. Keep in mind that a blueprint is a representation of something more tangible and real. It is not a one-size-fits-all tool. But it can be very helpful, even necessary, in moving forward.

After looking at hundreds of scrappy churches, we saw a pattern that was very common among all of these turnaround churches. The schematic is best presented as a continuous cycle. We call it the *Turnaround Cycle.*

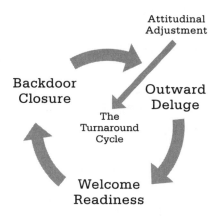

We will look at each of these points on the cycle. But, before we begin, let's look at attitudinal adjustment, since that is most often the starting point for church leaders. Frankly, the Turnaround Cycle is worthless without this prerequisite adjustment.

Attitudinal Adjustment

"I could not figure out where my attitude stunk the most," Ben confessed. We were interviewing the pastor to learn as much as we could about his turnaround church. He continued, "Some days, I would have the attitude of the victim. My church members don't support me. I can't compete with bigger churches. Our church doesn't have enough resources. I have to say, I had mastered the victim mentality."

Ben continued with helpful transparency: "On other days, I was mad. And I made a rear of myself at times. I would express my anger on Facebook. I wasted an incredible amount of time ranting on social media. There were days my wife told me I embarrassed her. Then I would get mad at her, and we would get in an argument. I was a miserable pastor and a miserable leader."

But Ben was in his eighth year serving as pastor of a turnaround church. The reversal began at year five, but he told us, "The real turnaround took place in my mind in the fourth year."

Now, that's fascinating verbiage. Ben had an attitudinal turnaround more than a year before the church had a visible turnaround. We asked him to give us details on exactly what took place.

"I heard a missionary speak," he said. His voice was subdued now. He reflected with quiet intensity. "I heard him speak about the persecuted church. I heard the sufferings he personally experienced. I heard how he buried his own son on the mission field in East Africa. And I heard how much he still loved the church, Christ's bride."

Ben paused, still in deep reflection. "I was ashamed," he said softly. "I was ashamed of both my attitude and actions. I had wasted time in self-pity and anger. I acted like I had problems while God was giving me my mission field right in front of my face. My heart was broken."

The story might be a bit more enjoyable if we could tell you that Ben's shift in attitude precipitated a massive turnaround in the church. And it might be more palatable if we could tell you he did not face critics and doubters. But we must be honest as we share about scrappy churches. Ben still had critics; he still does today. Ben still faced doubters; he still does today.

But what has changed is Ben's attitude and how he responds to these challenges. Ben was right. The turnaround began in his mind as he allowed the mind of Christ to guide him. You can't have a victim mentality with the mind of Christ. You can't conclude you have a shortage of resources with the mind of Christ. You can't live in anger with the mind of Christ.

The story of the scrappy church where Ben serves as pastor is neither sudden nor dramatic. When Ben became pastor, the church had an average worship attendance of 160, down from an historic high of 350 in the 1980s. For the first four years of his ministry, attendance continued a gradual decline to 135, and finally stabilized at that point for a year.

Now, in his eighth year as pastor, Ben has found joy and contentment. The church began to grow in his sixth year. Average attendance today is around 180. "I am happy with the growth," Ben told us. "But church health is more than attendance numbers. I am seeing God work through our congregation in a number of ways. We are making a difference. If our church were to disappear today, our neighborhood would miss us. In fact, many of our neighbors would grieve."

Ben smiled. "I couldn't say that a few years ago. If we had disappeared then, I don't think anyone outside our congregation would have noticed. That's not so today. We are really a neighborhood church making a difference."

In the previous chapter, we noted some of the transitions scrappy church leaders made. Let's look now at the five most common attitudinal adjustments we heard in our interviews and conversations.

They stopped making excuses. Many of the scrappy church leaders and members recalled how much energy and time they wasted making excuses. Those excuses would inevitably lead to lack of action.

Many of the excuses were common. We don't have enough resources. The people in our community would never be a part of our church. We don't have the right leaders. Our facilities are in terrible shape. We are too small to make a difference.

Scrappy church leaders and members moved from excuses to action. It was not always easy. In fact, it was rarely easy. But they made the attitudinal adjustment. And, over time, the fruit began to show.

They stopped blaming others. One of the most common sources of blame for pastors and other church leaders was the members themselves. The members in my church won't follow leadership. The members resist every change we try to make. The members won't do any of the work and ministry that has to get done. The members are a bunch of naysayers and critics.

One pastor told us the more he thought like that of the members, the worse they seemed to get. But, when he started viewing them through the lens of Christ, not only did his attitude change, but their attitude changed as well.

Other common sources of blame are other (usually bigger) churches, the denomination, the community, the culture, and the seminaries or Bible colleges. ("They didn't prepare me for this!") Scrappy church leaders issued a cease and desist order to themselves for playing the blame game. It does absolutely no good. It only makes matters worse.

They stopped comparing their church to others. One pastor said it well, "As long as I was comparing my church to others, I could never celebrate what God was doing in my church." Yes, we can learn from other churches, but that is different than comparing our church to them. There is a sharp distinction, or at least there should be, between learning from other churches and comparison.

Church comparison often results in a sense of inadequacy, jealousy, despondency, or anger. None of those four consequences are healthy at all! I really like what one church leader did when he saw his mind drifting toward comparisons. "When I drifted in that direction, I made a conscious effort to focus on how God was working in my church. I started using Philippians 4:8 as my guide."

They dealt with critics in a healthier way. It would be misleading to say that all of the scrappy church leaders are not bothered by critics. To the contrary, almost all of them said quite the opposite. Criticism still stinks. Critics still hurt.

There were three major themes I heard from scrappy church leaders and their responses to critics. First, they began to pray consistently for their critics. While the prayers did not always result in the transformation of the critic, they did result in the transformation of the scrappy church leader.

Second, they did not allow themselves to dwell on the criticisms. In my last meeting with Billy Graham before his death, I asked him how he dealt with criticism throughout his life and ministry. He simply said he did not allow himself to focus on the critics and their barbs. He just had to move forward.

The third theme is one we will unpack shortly. The scrappy church leaders made certain they spent as much of their time as possible in outwardly focused activities. The words of one of the leaders is telling: "While I never enjoy criticism, I am too focused on others and reaching the community to spend time dwelling on the critics. Having an inward focus is one of the worst things I can do as a leader."

They became continuous learners. This theme is becoming more and more apparent. Leaders of healthy and turnaround churches are seeking to learn every day. They read books. They attend conferences either in person or virtually. They are mentored. They are part of a learning community. Whenever our team hears a church leader say he or she is too busy to be involved in ongoing learning, we know that leader is not likely leading well.

Importantly, we often see this issue as a clear transition point in a turnaround church. The church leader makes the important decision to become a continuous learner. As the leader learns, the church benefits. As the church benefits, the church begins the process of the turnaround.

We rarely, if ever, see a scrappy church that does not have a leader who is a continuous learner. Indeed, that transition by the leader is often followed by the turnaround of the church.

A Need for Structure

Scrappy churches must have structure that allows them to continue to move forward. At a high level, structural effectiveness includes the right structure outwardly—*Outward Deluge*—the right structure for welcoming—*Welcome Readiness*—and the right structure for assimilation—*Backdoor Closure*. Let's examine each of these structures provided by the Turnaround Cycle in more detail.

Outward Deluge

Let's now return to the Turnaround Cycle and look at Outward Deluge. Those two words were chosen carefully for a reason.

First, it is a clear statement the church is focusing more on her community. The outward focus is the biblical response to both the Great Commission and the Great Commandment.

Second, the outward focus is a deluge, or flood, of efforts. As we have observed turnaround churches, we see outward efforts increase as much as fourfold. For example, if ten members in a church were spending one hour a week each ministering and reaching out to the community, that would mean the church is spending ten hours a week outwardly focused.

When that church becomes a turnaround church, the focus increases to forty or more hours a week, for example. Perhaps more people began to reach out to the community, or perhaps some of the members spend more time doing so, or both.

The point is a turnaround church, or scrappy church, does not shift its resources outwardly in an incremental fashion. They shift the resources *dramatically*. It is a deluge or flood in a new direction. Here are some examples of the Outward Deluge:

- The church leads the members in a systematic way to invite people in the community to church. We have a resource called Invite Your One to help guide churches (www.InviteYourOne.com).
- The church begins a major ministry in the community such as ESL (English as a Second Language) or partnership with a local public school.
- The church develops a ministry that addresses a significant problem in the community.
- The church trains members to have gospel conversations with people they encounter every day. One of the best books on this topic is *Turning Everyday Conversations into Gospel Conversations* by Jimmy Scroggins.
- The church uses its facilities for the community. Mark Clifton often shares the story of a turnaround church that used one of its larger rooms for birthday parties for kids in the community. Their parents absolutely loved it.

Obviously, the examples are endless. The point is, the church makes a significant shift in how its members spend their time. Sometimes, the church makes a similar, significant shift in its budgetary resources as well.

But it's not merely a shift. It's a deluge.

Welcome Readiness

As we continue on the Turnaround Cycle, the point of Welcome Readiness becomes very important. Welcome Readiness means the church is ready to receive guests who come to the worship services. It is a shame to do so much work to develop relationships in the community, only for them to have a bad experience when they visit our worship services.

Welcome Readiness is so much about our attitudes. We should prayerfully seek to see others as Jesus sees them. We should have a servant attitude toward our guests. We should rejoice at their presence, and let them know it.

Backdoor Closure

Backdoor Closure is all about assimilation. We reach out to the community. We welcome our guests. But we must do everything possible in God's power to keep them. We desire them to be a functioning part of the body of Christ (1 Cor. 12), rather than an occasional guest or an eventual dropout.

There is a lot to say about structural effectiveness for all three points on The Turnaround Cycle. It is vital for a scrappy church to become a turnaround church. I will walk you through each of these three critical issues in the next three chapters. But, first, allow me to address one more time the hope your church has.

Postscript: The Resurgence of the Neighborhood Church

As we unpack the details of what actually took place in scrappy churches, it could prove tempting to get lost in the details and to forget the big picture. And that big picture is the amazing reality that an increasing number of smaller and midsize churches are thriving, even in the supposed shadow of larger churches.

There is a revival of neighborhood churches. Your church address is not an accident. Indeed, I encourage you to read *Unexpected Comeback: The Surprising Return of the Neighborhood Church* by Sam Rainer, a book following the release of this book.

I write this postscript as a reminder of God's work in churches like yours. I write it as a reminder of the hope you have. And I write this reminder so you will remember the big picture. God is not done with your church. He is not done with your leadership.

Keep that big picture before you.

And now, let's look at the three major emphases of scrappy churches in the next three chapters.

1. http://hirr.hartsem.edu/American-Congregations-2015.pdf

CHAPTER 3

The Outward Deluge of Scrappy Churches

I MET ANTON MANY YEARS AGO. HE WAS ON STUDENT VISA from Russia, and it was his first time in the United States. Like any of us in a new culture, we don't fully understand matters those native to the culture take for granted. Such was the case when two of my friends and I took Anton to dinner.

The restaurant we chose had a "pick three" menu. You chose your salad, entrée, and dessert when you first ordered. We three Americans made our choices. Anton watched carefully as we ordered. It was his turn.

Like us three Americans, Anton made his choices. But, instead of ordering a salad, entrée, and a dessert, he ordered three entrees. The server was kind but clear, "Sir, you can't order those three." Anton looked hurt, "You mean I can't have those?"

I intervened. With likely misplaced compassion, I told the server it was okay. I would pay for his three entrees.

The orders came to our table.

Anton had three plates. On each plate respectively was a 14-ounce ribeye, a large grilled grouper, and a baked chicken. Two sides were included on each plate. For the mathematician, that's six total sides. There were also three desserts.

Anton stared at his plates for several long seconds. He then looked up.

In halting English he said, "I am unable to process what just happened."

Do you remember what I said earlier about the outward focus of scrappy churches? They typically increase their outward focus by fourfold or more. When I tell other leaders the same thing, they often stare blankly or look with their mouths agape.

It's as if they are saying the same words as Anton: "I am unable to process what just happened."

The idea of increasing our outward focus seems unreasonable, unlikely and, perhaps, impossible. But that is exactly what most of the scrappy churches did. But let's look at *how* these churches accomplished such a herculean task.

Let's return for a moment to the Turnaround Cycle. In its purist sense, a cycle is something that moves from point to point and keeps moving in that same direction. In the illustration of the Turnaround Cycle, the points on the cycle are

Outward Deluge, Welcome Readiness, and Backdoor Closure. For simplicity, I kept the cycle clean, as if we moved from one point to another.

But in real-life experiences, the path is not so clean and simple. Each of the points interacts with the others. For example, if you are leading your church toward Backdoor Closure, you are usually dealing with Welcome Readiness, and outwardly focused issues (Outward Deluge). Each point impacts the other points, either positively or negatively.

So our Turnaround Cycle might look more accurately like this depiction:

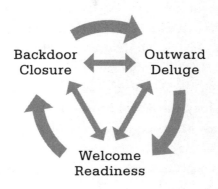

Okay, I know I've just made the illustration messy and hard to follow. My point, though, is simple. As we are dealing with one part of the cycle, we are usually dealing with all three. At the very least, how we deal with one part of the Turnaround Cycle impacts the other two parts.

Outward Deluge: Why Many Churches Struggle

Do you remember the fourfold factor I mentioned earlier? Simply put, most scrappy churches increased their outwardly focused effort by around four times. When I tell this to pastors of struggling churches, their responses are typically ones of disbelief.

"Wait a minute," one pastor from Colorado exclaimed. "I can't get my members to attend more than twice a month. That's just two to three hours a month! And now you are telling me we have to increase our time reaching the community by as much as four times. That's impossible!"

Okay, I get it. Many of you are stretched thin. Your members are busy, too busy. Life is hectic. Then someone tells you the church has to do more. You roll your eyes. You feel frustrated. You may feel more hopeless than ever. Allow me to address a couple of issues, two areas that might ease your concerns.

You need to lead the church to replace busyness with effectiveness. Look at your church calendar. Look at all the meetings on there. Look at the busyness every week. Are they all absolutely necessary? Be honest. Would your church suffer greatly if you began to eliminate some of the busyness of your church schedule?

I know. If you start eliminating things, you run the danger of conflict. Some of those activities and ministries are the metaphorical sacred cows. But I imagine some of them are just plain busyness. Can you eliminate some of those with minimal pain? Where is the low-hanging fruit? What can you stop doing now to make room for something better?

In many of our churches, we simply need to replace the good with great.

Go back to some of the attitudinal issues we addressed earlier. Is it possible you are the stumbling block toward eliminating busyness? Do you need to demonstrate both wisdom and courage? Life is too short to settle for mediocrity. Get started by leading your church to simplify and eliminate some of the busyness.

Your members will add capacity if they feel like they are doing something meaningful. Most everyone wants to be a part of something that makes a difference. Most everyone wants to make a difference. If your church's "active" members attend only twice a month, they possibly don't think their presence in the church makes a difference.

Keep in mind, your younger families will gladly do whatever is necessary to get their kids to soccer practice. That's really important for them. And for many of them, it is more important than attending church. Sure, we can find fault with them. We can express anger and frustration. Or we can offer them something more meaningful to do, something that makes a difference.

Also keep in mind, these younger families are part of the Millennial generation, those born between 1980 and 2000. They are the largest generation in America at 78 million strong. They and their children are a lot of people! We can make a difference as we seek to reach them.

That's what scrappy churches do.

That's what your church can do.

Let's look again at the Turnaround Cycle. Let's get serious about the Outward Deluge.

THE TURNAROUND CYCLE

Getting Scrappy with the Outward Deluge

You can't move incrementally when the church needs to turn around. Thus, we exhort church leaders to move toward a deluge or flood of outward ministry. That sounds good on paper, but how does it become a reality?

We first acknowledge there is no template for all churches. It is not a plug-and-play solution. But we can offer helpful categories. As you begin to think of how your church can become more outwardly focused in the community, look at three levels of focus: sustained, seasonal, and special. To be clear, scrappy churches do not choose one or two of the levels. They must be involved at *all* levels.

Sustained Outward Focus in Scrappy Churches

The church had an amazing ESL (English as a Second Language) ministry. For ten months out of the year, dozens of members participated in the ministry. Most of them were passionate about their work in this area. Susan told us, "I have never been involved in such a ministry. I meet people who have come to the United States for incredible reasons. They are from all over the world. It is an amazing experience."

But Susan thinks of the ESL ministry independently from the church. Even though they meet in the evenings at the church facilities, she has never invited any of the students to a worship service. She has not offered to take them to those services.

The ESL ministry is an incredible opportunity for the church to have a sustained outward focus. But it does not meet the definition of a sustained ministry because it is not intentionally connected to the rest of the church. So what is the definition of a sustained outward focus? It has four components.

1. *It involves a significant number of the church members.* You will have to decide your own definition of "significant," but it is more than the ministry of a small group in the church. The ministry is a draw for many members, because they can see it makes a difference. Many members eagerly participate in it. They see themselves making a difference in their work in the ministry.

2. *It is a year-round ministry.* A sustained outward focus is ongoing. Sure, the ministry may take breaks during the year, but it is operational most months. It is a relatively easy ministry to get lay volunteers who are willing to participate year-round because they are passionate about it.

3. *It is a part of the church's identity.* Because it is an ongoing ministry, many in the community define the church by the ministry. The church is "the ESL church." Another church is "the church that has the bread ministry in the community." And yet another church is "the church that has the recovery ministries."

4. *It is strategically and intentionally connected to the church.* This point is where many churches fail. Like the ESL ministry noted above, the church is not intentional about connecting those they serve to the entire congregation. Essentially, the church has a local congregation and a parachurch ministry on the side. Unfortunately, these two ministries often become competitive and conflicting rather than synergistic and integrated. In that sense, they can do more harm than good. A scrappy church makes certain its ongoing and sustained outreach is directly and integrally connected to the church. In the case of the ESL ministry, the members would be developing relationships to the point where they would naturally invite them to attend worship services or small groups with them.

I recently spoke to a pastor whose church is definitely a scrappy church. Its turnaround from decline to health is remarkable. He intuitively knew the church had to have an ongoing outward focus. He led the church to a basic but effective sustained outward focus. His church has ten adult Bible study classes. He asked each group to get creative and find ways to connect with the community and invite people to church on an ongoing basis.

The pastor's creativity led him to ask each of the ten groups to "adopt" one of ten months. Each group is now responsible for creatively inviting people to church for one month each. For now, they have no groups to cover July and November, but they have the other ten months covered.

"It has been amazing," the pastor told us. "I am not burdened with the responsibility of thinking how we can reach the community and invite folks. Instead, I unleash our members to come up with their own ways to do it. At the end of each of those ten months, I share from the pulpit what the class did for that month. It really has ignited our church, and it hasn't been a burden on any one person or group."

We asked the pastor how long this ministry has been in place. "We are halfway through our third year," he responded. "Some of the classes have repeated their outreach from previous years because they like it so much. Others have changed or tweaked theirs. They are all doing well."

The pastor had a twinkle in his eye as he continued. "I knew this ministry was doing well when I went into the grocery store a couple of months ago. The cashier said, 'Oh, you're the pastor of the inviting church.' That was music to my ears. We now have a reputation of being the church that opens our doors and invites people."

He had one more point he wanted to make. "You know, there is a large church just four blocks from our church," he said. "I used to be either intimidated or angry about that church. In fact, I had a hopeless feeling whenever I thought about it. Not anymore. There are plenty of people who need a church in our community. We may not ever be as large as the other church, but that's okay. God has both of our congregations here for a reason."

Do you get the picture of one of the major facets of the Outward Deluge? The scrappy churches have a sustained effort in reaching and inviting the community. Let's look at the second of the two components, the seasonal outward focus.

Seasonal Outward Focus in Scrappy Churches

Go get your attendance records.

Do you have them? Are you able to see month-by-month averages for the past couple of years? Maybe you have records for three or more years. That's even better.

If you are looking at monthly worship attendance averages, you will probably notice something right away. There are certain months when attendance dips. There are other months when attendance spikes.

Okay, if you aren't a numbers nerd like me, you might not have the precise statistics available, but you know intuitively when attendance will be higher or lower than normal. For example, church leaders shared with me some of their lower attendance months:

- "Two of our lower months are March and November. A week in March is spring break for most our schools. Our families take advantage of the break to go out of town. November is both fall break and Thanksgiving holidays. We have a lot of young people in our church, and they go visit family out of town for Thanksgiving."

- "It's June and July. Those two consecutive months stink. I think most of our church members take one or two weeks of vacation in those months. I have just come to expect it."

- "We actually have the entire summer as our low months. We have a lot of snow birds who have returned north, and we have many of our year-round church members who take vacations in the summer to go to cooler climates. Those two factors combined hit our attendance hard."

- "I can tell you the low attendance weeks ahead of time when the NFL schedule comes out. I look at the home games for our team and know a lot of folks will miss church because they are headed to the game. And we have several of our games with a kickoff time around noon."

Okay, you get the point. Now do the opposite exercise. Determine what your natural high attendance days are. The three most common in churches are:

- Easter. It's the family reunion time when all of the members show up on the same Sunday. You even get the once-or-twice-a-year attendees on Easter. I actually spoke to a young couple this past Easter at church who said these words without hesitation: "See you in a year." Ugh.

- Christmas Eve. Hear me well. *Please always have a Christmas Eve service.* It's the day where you are more likely to get the unchurched and non-Christians to attend. Your church is missing a great opportunity to reach people if it does not have a Christmas Eve service. Christmas still evokes warm memories for many people, even unbelievers. It is a time of celebration and tradition. It's just too important to skip.

- Mother's Day. The moms in your church typically want their husbands and children to attend church. Mother's Day is one of those days where the family actually yields to the wishes of the moms and wives. By the way, Father's Day is often a lower attendance day in churches. Go figure.

There could very well be several other days that are naturally high attendance days in your community. What are those days that naturally come to mind?

So what's the purpose of this exercise? It's a reminder that these natural high attendance days are seasonal in every church. It's a reminder of days when people are more likely to come to church. And it's a reminder that if receptivity to church is likely for them, it's likely for others as well.

Simply stated, your church's efforts to have an Outward Deluge should be both sustained and seasonal. In the cases we just noted, your church should make extraordinary effort at reaching your community for those high seasonal days. It's a time when biblically the fields are ready for harvest. Follow the words of Jesus Himself in John 4:35: "Listen to what I am telling you: Open your eyes and look at the fields, because they are ready for harvest."

What can you do on these seasonally high days of attendance? The possibilities are endless:

- Have a special emphasis on inviting people.
- Announce recognition of people, like moms on Mother's Day.
- Place paid ads on Facebook for the special days.
- Ask your members to have yard signs pointing to the special day.
- Make certain the home page of the church's website focuses on the special day. Remember the website is more for guests than members.

Scrappy churches will find ways to make the special day a truly inviting, gospel-centered, outwardly focused day. They will find ways to get it done rather than offering excuses.

Yes, scrappy churches will have a deluge of outwardly focused ministries. Some will be sustained and ongoing ministries. Some will be more seasonal in nature. Finally, some will be created by the church itself as a special emphasis. It is to that outward focus we turn.

Special Outward Focus in Scrappy Churches

Are you sensing the deluge of outwardly focused ministries of scrappy churches? Do you see that scrappy churches by their very nature are looking to do as much as possible to look beyond themselves? They create ongoing or sustained outwardly focused ministries. They take advantage of natural high-attendance days and seek to build upon them. And they also will create their own special emphases.

A special outward focus is a ministry created by a church that focuses on reaching beyond itself for a short-term emphasis. To be clear, the goal is not a mere high attendance day, but an opportunity to change the mind-set of its members. If they see good results from a short-term emphasis, they are more likely to reach out or invite someone naturally throughout the year.

Though I don't want to suggest the solutions to these challenges are programmatic, I do want to provide a programmatic solution as an example of a special outward focus.

Invite Your One (InviteYourOne.com) was created to provide a way to shift the mind-set of our members beyond spiritual naval gazing. Many scrappy churches have used this model with great success. The concept is simple. The members of the church formally commit to invite at least one person to church on a specific date. They actually share, through a commitment card, the name of their invited guest who has accepted to come to church on that day.

While Invite Your One does indeed have a high-attendance day effect, it is much more than that. When a church member sees that people are actually receptive to personal invitations (which they are), the member is more inclined to invite someone else in the future. That is why most churches see a residual positive impact beyond the designated Invite Your One day.

Here is a verbatim quote from a Cincinnati pastor who led his church in the special Invite Your One emphasis. He provided the quote in the forum we have at ChurchAnswers.com:

It was a great Sunday! We ended up with 429, which is incredible! (I thought we would be between 350 and 450 with a potential between 500–600). Before Invite Your One, our average was 260. The Sunday before Invite Your One we had 254 in worship attendance— Invite Your One 429! That's a 65 percent increase over our average attendance! The higher attendance was good—I enjoyed that—what pastor wouldn't? But what made my day was seeing my people bring their friends and family. They were coming up to me with a big smile saying, "Pastor, I got my one!" like they were surprised that it happened! I don't think I have ever—in over 20 years of pastoring—seen so many people engage in inviting folks! Also, I do think we had more first-time guests at our church than I have ever seen at one time, including many big days like Easter, where people come who are loosely affiliated with your church. Our Invite Your One was a completely different crowd—it was amazing! We had four people give their lives to Christ!

A pastor in the Denver area had similar growth on Invite Your One day, but it was the number of guests who continued to come that amazed him. "I was very excited on the day of Invite Your One, but I know how hype and excitement can quickly disappear. What has been most exciting is the number of guests we have each week has almost tripled for the seven months past Invite Your One. Our members really believe God is honoring their attempts to invite people to the church to hear the gospel."

Another great example of a special outward focus is a day honoring first responders: police, firefighters, emergency medical workers, and others. Such a day makes a huge statement to both the community and the congregation.

To be very clear, scrappy churches do not depend on a single or a few big events to reach people. It is simply part of a larger strategy toward Great Commission obedience. And in many scrappy churches, the strategy is working.

Scrappy Churches and the Deluge Factor

Scrappy.
Feisty.
Tenacious.
Determined.
Dogged.
Persistent.

Just a reminder: Scrappy churches do not give up. Their leaders do not give up. And their members (at least most of them) do not give up.

We have introduced you to the scrappy nature of these churches when it comes to reaching beyond themselves, to reaching their community. They have increased their outward focus many times over, often as much as four times more.

Scrappy churches have a *sustained* outward focus. Simply stated, they make sure they are reaching their community on a consistent year-round basis.

Scrappy churches have a *seasonal* outward focus. They find their naturally occurring higher attendance days and pour more time, effort, and, often, funds to reach even more people on those days.

Scrappy churches have a *special* outward focus. They seek to have at least one major effort a year that can be highly effective to reaching the community. We introduced you to the ministry called Invite Your One, but church leaders should not limit their ideas to just one program. Scrappy church leaders discover many special ways to reach their community.

Now you know why we call it *Outward Deluge*. The scrappy churches we found poured incredible efforts into reaching their community. And such efforts were not one-and-done. They persisted. They refused to give up. They were doggedly determined.

Kenneth serves as the pastor of a nondenominational church in Oregon. The church struggled for many years under his leadership. People told him to accept it. He was living in a tough time and a tough culture. But one day while reading the book of Acts, it hit him. He says God got him. The early churches did not have an easy time. They were in difficult cultures. "So I asked myself as I read Acts," he said, "why is it any different today? Don't we serve the same God with the same power and the same possibilities?"

Kenneth began to pray for opportunities to reach the community. He got a few members to join him in those prayers. Soon Kenneth and the few members began intentionally connecting with people in the community. Then other members joined them. Then even more members joined them. God was moving this church, and most of the people in the congregation did not want to miss what He was doing.

After about six months, Kenneth said, "We were flooding the community with different types of outreach ministries." Sounds a little bit like Outward Deluge, doesn't it? The church is seeing the fruit of their obedience. For the first time in over a decade, the church in Oregon is reaching people. It is growing. It is indeed growing in a healthy way.

But Kenneth and the members realized soon they needed to make certain their church was a truly welcoming church. They began to make changes to be friendlier, to be more welcoming, and to be better prepared for the guests who were coming.

On the Turnaround Cycle, we call that *Welcome Readiness.*

It is the subject of the next chapter.

Chapter 4

Scrappy Churches Are Welcoming Churches

THE SECRET GUEST.

It sounds a bit mysterious, maybe like the CIA for churches. But it's really one of the most helpful tools I've ever used or seen.

The concept is simple. You recruit someone who has never been to your church to visit your church. Perhaps you offer them a $50 gift card for their efforts. You ask them to attend your church and pay careful attention to everything they see and experience. In fact, it's even better if they complete a secret guest survey. We've made one available for you at the end of this book. You can also get a digital copy of the Secret Guest Survey at ThomRainer.com/scrappychurch.

Make certain you tell them to be brutally honest. You want to know the good, the bad, and the ugly.

If appropriate, take the guest to a meal or to coffee within a couple of days of their visit. Let them go over the survey point by point. Listen carefully. Don't interrupt them unless you need clarification. Soak it in. Even if it's painful, soak it in.

We call this process "looking in the mirror." And to be clear, it's not always a fun and enjoyable process.

Frankly, I don't like looking in the mirror at myself. Our bathroom has a lot of lights. It has too many lights. I am able to see myself very clearly. It's not a pretty picture. I really look a lot older than I think I am. And though I've never considered myself handsome, those lights and that big mirror remind me again and again that I am both old and ugly.

Ugh. I really don't like mirrors.

So why would you put yourself through the pain of looking in the mirror for your church? It's pretty simple. You can't improve unless you know the areas you need to improve.

And scrappy churches are constantly seeking to improve.

Bruce is the pastor of a scrappy church. Like the other scrappy churches mentioned in this book, his church is an example of a turnaround church. Many deemed it an impossible turnaround church. Faith Church is in a transition neighborhood. In fact, the neighborhood has been in some type of transition for over twenty years. And like many neighborhood churches, Faith Church has not handled the transitions well.

The glory days of the church were more than twenty-five years ago when worship attendance hit its peak of 325. Just a few years ago, the attendance dipped below 75. Many in the church thought closure was imminent. And Bruce admits he was among them.

"I had given up," he told us. "Yeah, I really thought closure was inevitable. Honestly, I was working on my own exit plan."

We were obviously curious. The church was in a healthy recovery. After three scrappy years, attendance was more than 120. Hope was back. The gloom-and-doom attitude of earlier years had been replaced with God-given optimism and excitement. So, we asked the obvious question: What happened?

"I read your book *Breakout Churches*," he told us. "That book was a wake-up call for me. You told the story of churches on the verge of death that turned around. I thought if those churches could reverse the negative trends, my church could as well. But I wondered how we could see ourselves in the mirror accurately to know we had to make major changes."

There was the phrase again: "see ourselves in the mirror." We asked what his first step was.

"I asked an unchurched person to visit our church," Bruce responded. "I asked him to give us the truth, good or bad. I wanted to know what others saw when they came to our church for the first time."

What did he see? We were waiting for Bruce's response with anticipation.

"It was absolutely terrible," he recalls. "Man, it was brutal. I can't remember one good thing he said, but I remember his closing word: 'I couldn't leave your church fast enough.'"

Wow. Those words hurt just hearing them. But Bruce decided to take the negative report and see how God would make it positive. He brought key leaders together and presented the secret guest report to them.

"There was this awkward moment of silence after they read the report," he recalls. "Then the chairman of the elders spoke up. He said he knew the church was dying, but he had no idea the death was the result of self-inflicted wounds."

It was that moment, Bruce said, when the leadership decided they would no longer be passive. "If our church was going to die," he said, "we would die trying to make a difference. That was the turning point. No, we didn't have a sudden turnaround. It's been slow and tough. But it has happened. We are one scrappy church."

Scrappy church.

Determined.

Tenacious.

Tough.

Never give up.

The Welcoming Church on the Turnaround Cycle

Backdoor
Closure

Outward
Deluge

**Welcome
Readiness**

Scrappy churches are typically focused on one point on the Turnaround Cycle. In the case of Faith Church, it took the wake-up call of a secret guest to cause them to start looking at other points on the cycle like Outward Deluge and Backdoor Closure. The members and leaders of the church had to look in the mirror to know they had to make major changes.

Indeed, Faith Church had to grasp it was not ready for guests before it could ever move in the direction of a greater outward focus.

So, what are some of the common issues guests have when they visit a church? We asked that question not too long ago and got a lot of responses. Here are the top ten I noted in my earlier book, *Becoming a Welcoming Church*:

1. *The stand-and-greet time in the worship service was unfriendly and awkward.* When I first saw this response coming in by the hundreds, I was surprised. And as I dug deeper, I discovered there were two issues with the stand-and-greet time. First, some guests just felt awkward with the exercise. It seemed to be a ritual more for the members than the guests. Second, a number of guests did not mind the stand-and-greet time, but they felt left out during the welcome. Either they were totally ignored, or they were inundated with what they perceived were superficial greetings.

2. *Unfriendly church members.* Most church members do not view themselves as unfriendly. But they do not see themselves from the perspective of church guests. They don't usually speak to them because they don't know them. And the church members usually retreat to the comfort of the holy huddles of the people they do know.

3. *Unsafe and unclean children's areas.* This response generated the most emotional comments. If your church does not have clear safety and security procedures, and if the children's area does not appear clean and

sanitary to the guests, do not expect young families to return to your church. Indeed, as word about your children's area grows, do not expect young families to visit the first time.

4. *No place to get information on the church.* Guests are trained by their experiences to look for a central welcoming and information center. But here is the catch. Some churches did not have any such information center. Some churches did have them, but you couldn't find them. And some churches have them in good visible locations, but they had no one manning the center. Guests told us they were hesitant to go to an unmanned welcome center. The church might as well not have an information and welcome center if no one will be there to help guests.

5. *Bad church website.* Most of the church guests went to the church website before they attended a worship service. Even if they decided to visit the church after looking at a bad website, they visited the church with a negative disposition. The two critical items guests want to see on a church website are the physical address of the church and times of the services. It's just that basic. Keep in mind this reality. The church website is the front door of the church. Will guests feel welcome when they come to the door?

6. *Poor signage.* If you have been attending your church a few weeks, you don't need signage. But guests do. And they get frustrated when they don't have clear directional signage for parking, for the entrance to the worship center, for the children's area, and others.

7. *Insider church language.* Listen to the words in the worship service of your church. Listen to the announcements. Listen to the sermon. Listen to the casual conversations. Are members saying things that a first-time guest would not understand? Well, that's what church guests told us. They said they went into some churches thinking that much of the language was foreign and filled with acronyms.

8. *Boring or bad church services.* My surprise was not that this factor made the top ten; it was that it was only listed as the eighth most frequent concern. In the past, church leaders of small churches would tell me they don't have the resources for quality services. In the digital age with so many affordable resources, no church is allowed that excuse.

9. *Members telling guests they were in the wrong pew or chair.* I thought this rude and insensitive behavior disappeared years ago. The church guests told us otherwise. In fact, the most common comment was, "You are sitting in *my* pew." Unbelievable. Totally unbelievable.

10. *Dirty facilities.* Some of the comments were brutal: "Didn't look like it had been cleaned in a week." "No trash cans anywhere." "Restrooms were worse than a bad truck stop." "Pews had more stains than a Tide commercial." You get the picture. A dirty church communicates to the guest, "We really don't care."

You can read the full picture of Welcome Readiness in *Becoming a Welcoming Church.* For the purpose of looking at scrappy churches, we need to examine this point specifically on the Turnaround Cycle.

Keep in mind, the Turnaround Cycle in scrappy churches has three main emphases: Outward Deluge, Welcome Readiness, and Backdoor Closure. Though the cycle depicts movement from one point to another, it's better visualized as emphasis on one point, but not to the exclusion of the other points.

Simply stated, each point on the Turnaround Cycle affects the other. If you get a lot of people coming to your church with an Outward Deluge, they won't return if they are treated poorly, that is, if your church is not prepared with Welcome Readiness. And you will certainly have Backdoor Closure problems if you don't reach them and welcome them in the first place.

In a recent overview of scrappy churches, I asked their leaders for specific changes they made toward Welcome Readiness. When it was all said and done, I was able to put the changes into three buckets.

Bucket #1: Attitudinal Change

Jerome was beginning year three serving his church as pastor. The third year is often the most difficult year for pastors. The honeymoon was over. The initial surge of excitement about the new pastor had transformed to day-to-day routines. And complacency had crept back into the church.

"The change was palpable," Jerome told us. "The excitement had diminished, and many of the members had reverted back to their me-first mentality. I had been in ministry long enough to know we would soon go from complacency to infighting. It happens every time the members start focusing on their own desire and preferences."

What did he do? "Well, I thought about it and prayed about it for a few days," Jerome responded. "I looked for something straightforward—low-hanging fruit, if you will."

Jerome, in fact, used the secret guest survey we created. "The timing was great. You had just come out with the survey, and I needed something to change attitudes at the church," he explained. Then his eyes widened and he smiled softly. "It was a perfect solution. I knew it could be a wake-up call for our church, a desperately needed wake-up call."

Jerome sought the counsel of a respected elder, Bartley. He explained, "Bartley has two characteristics I really needed. First, he is a man of total integrity. I never question his word or his character. Second, he's a straight shooter. He doesn't mince words. I really needed someone who would help me move forward with this project."

So, the pastor shared the idea with his trusted elder. He explained the concept of the secret guest. Someone would visit the church and write on a survey their experiences and opinions. But Bartley was so enthused about the idea that he wanted to take it a step further.

Jerome explained, "Bartley not only wanted to move forward with the secret guest, he wanted the guest to report back to our leaders. And he had a person in mind right away. Her name is Sally, and she is vice president of human resources at the corporation where Bartley works. Bartley had been trying to get Sally and her husband to come to church, but they had no desire to come."

The pastor continued the story: "Bartley knew Sally would take the challenge of trying to help us improve the church. She had a zeal for organizational improvement. Bartley also knew it was the perfect opportunity to get a non-Christian to church. He saw all kinds of upsides in the project."

Sally indeed visited the church. As expected with her driven personality, she poured over the secret guest survey ahead of the visit. When she arrived, she was in full assessment mode. She took meticulous mental and written notes.

But the process did not end there. Bartley had invited Sally to bring her report to the elders, the deacons, and more than a dozen other leaders in the church. Sally seemed to relish the task.

"It was both exciting and painful to hear Sally's report," Jerome told us. "She was an incredible presenter and had a thorough visual presentation as well. She blew us away with her zeal and thoroughness."

He continued, "She also hit us over the head with her observations. She saw things we never see: dirty restrooms, bad signage, difficult parking, and nonchalant greeters. But the words that hit us the hardest were, 'You are among the rudest people I've ever been around.' That stung! We all thought we were pretty friendly. We told her so, and she didn't mind the pushback at all." Jerome paused for a moment, and then continued the narrative.

"She was never unkind," Jerome interjected, "but she was about as straight talking as I've ever heard. Sally explained how the only friendliness she encountered was superficial friendliness. She called it 'fake friendliness,' a take on fake news. She told us it looked like we were trying to be friendly instead of really being friendly. I remember her words that stung the most, 'Many of you seemed like you had to be friendly because you are a Christian.'"

Ouch.

But the good news is how the church responded. Instead of being defensive, instead of blaming others, instead of shooting the messenger, the leaders took the report to heart. It caused them to look in the mirror, to see themselves as an outsider saw them.

Please see their response clearly. See what they did so we can learn from them.

> This congregation showed the clear signs of a scrappy church.
>
> Instead of blaming others, they sought to make the corrections in their own hearts.
>
> Instead of bemoaning their lack of resources, they saw their greatest resources to be their own attitude.
>
> Instead of wallowing in pity at a scathing report, they saw it as an opportunity to change and move forward.

The pastor noted that the changes were both dramatic and immediate. "You could tell the difference the next Sunday," he exclaimed. "People came to church with a new attitude. They had real smiles on their faces. They helped each other and they reached out to guests."

Such is the persistent nature of a scrappy church. Their first step in Welcome Readiness is a change in attitude or a renewed attitude. It doesn't affect the budget. It hardly takes any more time. It's not a new program or new ministry. It's simply a commitment to look in the mirror, to see the church from the perspective of the outsider.

That leads to the second bucket of Welcome Readiness: a change in actions.

Bucket #2: Actionable Change

I like the way Marty put it: "Don't start changing actions until you start changing hearts." Marty is the lead pastor of a six-year-old church in Colorado. "We started gung-ho," he said with a wry smile. "But it didn't take us long to start acting like an established church. We got set in our ways after our second year. We drifted to that inward focus you often talk about. But I didn't do anything about it for a couple of years. Not a good move on my part."

Mountain Creek Church is a classic scrappy church. It is a normative size church of about 125 in attendance. Like most congregations, the church drifted inwardly without an explicit Great Commission focus. Like most congregations, the church really did not recognize its drift at first.

The story of Mountain Creek Church is one with a good ending, at least at this point. We could share powerful stories of their turnaround at every point of the Turnaround Cycle. Indeed, we could point to great examples of what the church did at the point of Welcome Readiness alone. But let's take a moment and look at only the actionable items they did to get ready for guests.

Before we go further, I want you to note the total cost of all the improvements they made: $0. That's right, here was a church that needed to take several action steps to have a healthy welcoming ministry, but they had no budget funds to do it.

But they made it work.

That is, by definition, what a scrappy church does.

New welcome center. Church members built the welcome center from barn scrap lumber. The lumber was donated by a neighbor of a member. Several men and women in the church worked on a Saturday to build the center with signage. It looks absolutely incredible in all of its vintage beauty. In fact, it has become a point of fascination and conversation by guests who see it for the first time.

New signage. There was plenty of scrap lumber to make new signs for the parking lot, the entrances, and the interior. In fact, it looks really cool with the rough vintage theme. There was a cost for the paint, but a church member made the purchase. In the process of trying to find someone to paint the signs, the church discovered they had an artist in their membership. She did an incredible job painting the lettering on each sign.

Updated bathrooms. The church has four bathrooms. They were in pretty sad shape. A leader in one of their small groups, called community groups, challenged three other community groups to "adopt" a bathroom. Members of the four community groups spent an entire Saturday painting and providing cosmetic updates to all of the bathrooms. Each of the groups paid for and supplied their own materials at a nominal cost.

Informational church brochures. The church has a very nice four-color brochure to give to guests and new members. Again, they had no budget to pay for their printing. The church did something I have not seen very often. They secured sponsors, four in all, for the brochures. I understand any possible objection, such as commercializing the church. But, when you are a scrappy church, you have to make some out-of-the-box moves. The church also secured a single sponsor for their guest cards.

Loaves of bread to give to guests. Phoebe took the lead here. She is an incredible volunteer at the church. She went to Panera Bread and asked them what they did with their leftovers on Saturday nights. They told her they threw them away. She asked if she could have them. After a formal application, they said "yes." Now the church has bread to give guests, bread for church members, bread to give as outreach in the community, and bread for a pregnancy center in the community. Total cost is, of course, zero.

A redesigned website. The church's website is the front door for the church. It's where prospective guests will first visit. They will look for the times of the services. They will get the physical address of the church to enter into their GPS. If they have young children, they will check to make sure it's a good place to bring their kids. To be transparent, this redesigned site did cost a few dollars, but not much. And the person in the church who redesigned it as a ministry also picked up all the costs. The church did not pay anything for the redesign.

Do you get the picture? Do you see how these churches didn't see obstacles, just opportunities? Do you understand the scrappy nature of what they do? Do you grasp how they really believe all things are possible through God?

Bucket #3: Assimilation Change

Before we leave this point on the Turnaround Cycle, we need to look at one more critical factor in Welcome Readiness: assimilation change. Stated simply, too many churches neglect the follow-up of guests. Yet that may be one of the most critical factors in the scrappy church.

Certainly, the church needs to have an attitudinal change and to take the necessary actions to complement and augment the attitudes. But the church cannot merely welcome people and forget about them. The congregation must follow-up or assimilate them. Though we could spend volumes talking about assimilation of guests, let's look at the two most effective scrappy approaches churches take.

First, they are intentional about developing relationships with guests. Yeah, I know. That's stating the obvious. But, frankly, most churches aren't doing the obvious. One church has three families who have taken on the role of inviting guests to lunch after the worship services. Listen to what Tim said about his ministry.

"My wife and I see this as a part of our ministry at the church," he explained with obvious enthusiasm. "Even just after one lunch, we usually see great results. In fact, it's probably the best follow-up ministry in our church. Our pastor was doing most of it before we got involved, and it was wearing him out. We really love the ministry. It may cost us a few dollars, but it is well worth it."

For sure, there are many ways for members to develop relationships with guests, but the lunch invitation is one of the most effective and easiest to do. You simply invite them. "We are amazed how many people accept our invitation," Tim said with his contagious laugh. "My wife and I thought it would be the exception when someone said, 'yes.' We have found the exception is when they say, 'no.'"

The second most common approach to assimilating guests is encouraging them to get in small groups, or life groups, or home groups, or Sunday school classes, or community groups, or whatever you call them. In many ways, this approach is an extension of developing relationships, but it is powerful because the relationship is ongoing.

Scrappy churches really see and promote the value of groups. The leaders take every opportunity to highlight their importance. The groups are celebrated and given the spotlight on a regular basis. In fact, it is a much bigger factor than assimilating guests; it is one of the biggest factors in assimilating *everyone* in the church. We will look at that issue and many others in the next chapter, "Scrappy Churches Close the Back Door."

To that point of the Turnaround Cycle we now turn.

CHAPTER 5

Scrappy Churches Close the Back Door

ALLOW ME TO SHOW MY AGE FOR A MOMENT.

I remember when my parents got central air conditioning in our small home. It was a pretty big deal. I had never heard of central air conditioning. But now we had it. And I really liked it.

We had to make adjustments to this new lifestyle, to say the least. First, my mom declared she was in charge of the thermostat. No one was to touch it except her. Second, we had to do things differently with our doors, especially during the summer season. Let me explain.

The summers were notoriously hot and sticky in my south Alabama hometown. You could feel the thickness of the heat twenty-four hours a day. Prior to the central air conditioning, we had a small window unit that hardly made a dent in cooling the house. Our main defense was big fans in every room and the strategic opening of two doors: the front door and the back door.

The opening of the doors, for certain, put us at the mercy of the speed and the direction of the wind. But at those moments where we could catch the wind just right, the breeze would blow through our home with gusts of precious cooling. We always kept the front and back door open for that very reason. We hoped for a cool breeze to give us a momentary reprieve from the sweltering heat.

But when we got central air conditioning, our habits had to change. We had to keep both doors closed to keep the cool temperatures in the house. And you can probably guess who was the worst offender about closing the doors. Yep, I was at fault more than anyone in the family. I always left the house through the back door. And for months I failed to adjust my habits to the new reality of air conditioning. I kept the back door open.

It took a conversation and a threat from my dad to change my habits. My dad was a man of few words, so his stern conversations were not pleasant at all. Even more, he promised to start taking my weekly allowance to pay toward the electric bill if I persisted in my offense. I was devastated. How could I make it without my one dollar of weekly compensation?

Dad's words were simple but forceful: "Shut the back door, son. You are letting all the cold air out."

I finally learned my lesson. I shut the back door. We kept the cold air in the house.

How People Go Out the Back Door at Your Church

At its basic level, the back door is open two different ways in your church. First, the most commonly known is simply people leaving the church. They drop out altogether, or they move their membership to another church. For years, we thought of the back door in this manner.

But we are increasingly becoming more aware of another way people leave the back door of our churches: less frequent attendance. This type of exodus is more difficult to gauge and address because members are not actually leaving. They are just not showing up as frequently. Let's look at this matter with an oversimplified illustration.

Let's suppose First Community Church has one hundred members, and they all attend every Sunday for a year. The math is simple. The church obviously has an average attendance of one hundred.

But now let's suppose the church has an unfortunate split. Exactly fifty members leave or, in line with our metaphor, go out the back door. The rest continue to attend faithfully. The church's average attendance is now fifty.

In a town of close proximity is Second Community Church. It too has one hundred members. For a year, the members attend every Sunday, and the average attendance is one hundred. But, in the next year, the members' commitment wanes. Instead of attending every Sunday, they attend, on the average, every other Sunday. The average attendance thus drops to fifty.

Two churches in two communities. Both churches have a starting point of the same number of members and faithful attendance. But, in a year, attendance is cut in half in both churches for two very different reasons. First Community Church loses half its members. Second Community Church loses no one, but the members attend with less frequency.

To be clear, both scenarios are harmful to the church. Both scenarios result in attendance cut in half. But each scenario is significantly different than the other.

Both First Community Church and Second Community Church have a backdoor problem. And though the reasons for the problem are different, the solutions are similar. We know they are similar because we have heard that from scrappy churches.

Scrappy Churches and the Back Door

The Church at Jamesville is a scrappy church by almost any definition. It went from decline to growth in attendance numbers but, just as importantly, the overall health of the church is so much better by any standard.

Like the other churches in this book, The Church at Jamesville clearly followed the Turnaround Cycle. It definitely experienced an Outward Deluge. Likewise, the church made incredible strides toward Welcome Readiness. But the story upon which I would like to focus for this church is its amazing turnaround at the point we call Backdoor Closure.

Once again, The Turnaround Cycle is oversimplified, but it does help us to see visually the three main emphases of scrappy churches. In the case of The Church at Jamesville, their story of Backdoor Closure is worth retelling.

The church was doing fairly well reaching people and welcoming them to the worship services. Indeed, there was a palpable excitement among the members as they saw their church take on a new life and excitement. But the pastor, Kevin, was not happy with some of the developments in the turnaround.

"Don't get me wrong," Kevin began. "I was very grateful to see our church begin to reach people in the community and to welcome them to our church. That was definitely so much better than the apathy of our past. The problem was our attitude of 'one-and-done.' We invited them once and gave them a nice welcome to the church, and that was it. People were coming in, but they weren't sticking."

Kevin realized the problem was bigger than guest retention. In fact, most of the church's decline over the past few years had been related to backdoor issues of the members as well. "We were just seeing people slowly fade away from the church," Kevin said.

So the pastor made a major and critical decision. He would become the leader of their life groups. "We had fewer than 25 percent of our adults in life groups," Kevin told us. "I knew we had a big assimilation problem, and I knew part of the problem was our lack of emphasis on our life groups. I thought the biggest statement I could make about our groups was becoming the leader of them."

Kevin made life groups a major focus of his ministry and of the church's ministry. His passion and vision were contagious. When you walked in the lobby, you saw descriptions of each life group. There was clear and obvious verbiage welcoming anyone to join a group.

The pastor mentioned the life groups regularly in the worship services. They were also a major emphasis in the new members' class where Kevin encouraged the prospective members to get involved in a group right away.

Additionally, Kevin began monitoring the attendance numbers in the life groups. He resisted this path at first. "I really cringed when I would hear pastors talk about their numbers incessantly," Kevin explained. "I was determined to have a healthier focus, so I almost disregarded numbers altogether. You might say I threw the baby out with the bathwater."

His attention to the attendance of the life groups was not for the sake of undue focus on numbers, but to monitor the health of the church. "I realized that if there was a single health indicator for our church health, it was life group attendance," Kevin told us. Those in life groups were more likely to share the gospel, more likely to give more, more likely to be involved in ministry and, of course, more likely to attend worship services."

Kevin is a classic scrappy church pastor. He demonstrated his tenacity in a number of ways, not the least of which was his emphasis on life groups. "Look," he said bluntly, "we began closing the back door with our emphasis on life groups. I would be crazy to do otherwise."

We need more pastors and church leaders with Kevin's heart and attitude. To be clear, from Kevin's perspective, the process was often tedious, often exhausting, and often subject to criticism. "You know, as I sit here talking to you," he pondered in our interview, "it's easy to act like I just pushed a lot of buttons and things happened. But that's not the case. I wore myself out at times. It was really three steps forward and two steps backward."

Such is the common theme in all of these scrappy churches. The leaders are typically busy taking small steps and making incremental progress. They don't see the gains their churches are making. Only in the clear view of 20/20 hindsight do they realize how God was and is using them.

Unfortunately, many of them give up before they have the joy of seeing the fruit of their labors. Typically, the process takes years, not months. Scrappy church leaders are not only persistent; they persevere as well.

Keep in mind, we are providing an example of one pastor in one scrappy church at one point on the Turnaround Cycle focusing on one thing: life groups. Let's return to the point of the Turnaround Cycle called Backdoor Closure. Are there some key commonalities among the scrappy churches that were successful closing the back door? Indeed, there were four commonalities. Let's look at each of them.

Backdoor Closure #1: High Expectations

"If you expect much, you will get a lot more than if you expect nothing."

The comment came from a scrappy church pastor. It is profound in its simplicity and transparency.

"I have served as pastor of two churches in the past eleven years," he shared with us. "If there has been a common theme to my leadership, it's been an overabundance of caution. I have led from a posture of either fear of failure or fear of conflict."

He continues, "As a result, I have led expecting little of our members. I really didn't know how to communicate expectations, nor did I know what expectations to put forth. And if I ever got clarity on some ideas to put on the table, I usually kept my mouth shut for fear of criticisms."

The next words from the pastor were powerful. "I finally came to a point in my life and ministry where I was tired of leading defensively," he said. "This life is too short to lead from fear and caution. I asked God to give me strength and wisdom to begin leading my church—I mean really leading my church."

Some of the more seasoned church members began to notice a change in the pastor's conversations and leadership. He would speak from the pulpit and in informal conversations about the importance of community groups, of being involved in a ministry through the church, and of being a joyful giver. His posture was not one of legalism or rigidity, but one of joy from being involved in God's work. Though the pastor never used the phrase "scrappy church" until we spoke with him, he readily identified with the term.

"I love it!" he exclaimed. "That's exactly what we are. We are a scrappy church. We are in the shadow of two large churches. We don't have the best facilities in the world. Our neighborhood has a lot of transition taking place. But we still are making a difference. Yep, we are scrappy."

Not all the church leaders could point with specificity to a precise moment when their churches became scrappy churches, but this leader could. It began at the moment he decided to lead with boldness and courage rather than fear and defensiveness. And the first indication of his new leadership enthusiasm was a clear statement about high expectations in the church.

That issue raises an obvious question. Exactly what does it mean to have high expectations in the church?

In this chapter we will look at the primary ways a high expectation church demonstrates expectations, particularly in groups and a new members' class. For now, the key issue to grasp is that high expectations are first an attitude. Listen to the words of Phil, the pastor of a scrappy church in the panhandle of Florida.

"One of the exercises that woke me up toward my attitude about church leadership was reading all of Paul's letters in the New Testament with a specific lens," he began. "I wanted to see what Paul really expected of all those churches he encouraged or admonished."

What did Phil see?

"Well, it was eye-opening, to say the least," he responded. "Don't get me wrong. I know I'm not the apostle Paul, and I know Paul wasn't the pastor of the churches. But I did learn in a powerful way that Paul made no apologies for expected attitudes and behaviors of church members. I knew I had to go a long way in changing my leadership style."

We also asked Phil if he encountered any bumps or obstacles as he began to articulate greater expectations for his church members.

"You bet I did," he said resolutely. "To be clear, I think I did everything I could to get buy-in, and not to run roughshod over people. I didn't want to move from one extreme to another, from passive leadership to autocratic leadership. So, I tried to move slowly enough to bring our members along. But you know how it goes. It was change and some people just don't deal with change very well."

As Phil continued his conversation, we heard a theme that became common among scrappy church leaders: They don't want to live their lives in mediocrity.

"I was to the point I either needed to quit the ministry or change my leadership," Phil said bluntly. "I knew God had called me to this ministry, and I had no sense He called me out of it. I didn't want to live my life mired in mediocrity. It was time for me to change, even though I knew I would pay a price."

Obviously, the scrappy church pastors made changes in their attitudes. Those new attitudes most often resulted in a new commitment to raise the bar in the church, or to lead the church toward high expectations. Though the new higher expectations took several different paths, the most common new or renewed emphases focused on groups, ministry involvement, and new member classes.

Backdoor Closure #2: Groups

One of the single most powerful tools toward Backdoor Closure is getting people involved in groups. As we noted earlier, groups come in a variety of names, from life groups to community groups to home groups to Sunday school classes and more.

Groups are relational connection points, and relationships are among the greatest sticky factors. Groups have inherent accountability; you know when someone is absent, hurting, or struggling. Groups are simply people learning together and doing life and ministry together.

As a Pennsylvania pastor of a scrappy church told us, "If I could start my ministry over, I would have a greater emphasis on moving people to community groups. I just did not lead well in that area early in my ministry."

Scrappy churches do not have the funds for expensive resources and facilities. They understand, however, that the basics of ministry are powerful without the extras and niceties. "Our church has a small and tight budget," said Len, a pastor from Missouri. "In the past I used that as an excuse for our church not to minister and to reach people. I guess God got ahold of me. My eyes began to see possibilities I did not see before."

Len continues: "I made a list of adults I believed were my most committed church members. Out of an attendance of 130 adults and children, I came up with a list of 41 adults. As I looked over the list, I tried to discern what they had in common. Then it hit me. Everyone on that list was active in one of our life groups. Every single one."

It was a powerful wake-up call for Len. "I didn't have to have thousands of dollars or state-of-the-art facilities. I just needed to lead our church to increase the importance of our life groups. It's made a huge difference the past two years."

Backdoor Closure #3: Ministry Involvement

Scrappy churches get it. If the members are involved in ministry, they are more likely to stay with the church for the long haul. But, as Jason notes, it's not just about closing the back door.

"For sure, getting people involved in ministry through our church has been great for assimilation," he told us, "but I see even greater benefits. For example, our financial secretary told me that those who are volunteers or involved in ministry are our most faithful givers. I can also tell you those same people have incredible attitudes as a whole. The bottom line is ministry involvement means better assimilation, better giving, and greater unity in the church. It's huge for our church."

Once again, note the pattern of scrappy churches. They stay with the basics. They don't try to have all the amenities some of the larger churches may have. And they don't make excuses for what they don't have.

We were curious how these scrappy churches got new members involved in ministry. If ministry involvement is so important for assimilation, it has to be critical for the new member. He or she needs to be involved immediately, if possible.

The most common ministry involvement for new members was the greeters' ministry, sometimes called the hospitality ministry, and sometimes called the welcoming ministry. This ministry is great for new members. The new member is typically enthused about the ministry of the church, because he or she just joined. The ministry is also an easy entry point. Most of those who get involved get the essence of the ministry within a short time. As I noted earlier in this book, I wrote *Becoming a Welcoming Church* as an overview for all church members, including those in the welcoming ministry.

Steve, a pastor from central Ohio, reminded us of an important factor in getting members involved in ministry. "If you don't have a process in place," he said, "it will fall through the cracks. I know we can encourage people to be involved in ministry, and it can happen organically. But, most of the time, we aren't intentional about getting people in our different ministries. We have to have some type of process in place for it to have ongoing effectiveness."

Of course, we asked Steve how his church moved members into ministry. His response was quick: "If it doesn't begin in the new members' class, it probably won't happen." Thanks, Steve. You provided us a good segue into the fourth key of Backdoor Closure. Let's look at the new members' class.

Backdoor Closure #4: The New Members' Class

Back in the 1990s, when I was traveling around the country doing conferences on closing the back door, I would mention the importance of a new members' class for assimilation. I became accustomed to seeing blank stares. Fewer than one of the ten attendees at these conferences had a new members' class in their church. It sure is a different story today. These classes are now commonplace.

To be clear, though, not all new members' classes are of equal quality or caliber. The mere existence of these classes does not guarantee they will be effective in closing the back door. Here is where the scrappy churches made certain they did make a difference.

As we spoke to different leaders of scrappy churches, we noted several commonalities about their new members' classes. Here are a few:

- The pastors of the scrappy churches made sure the new members' class, by whatever name they called it, was a persistent high priority in the church. Noted Robin, a pastor in Minnesota: "I made certain I said something about the class to the entire church two or three times a month. They knew it was important in the life of our congregation."

- The classes were a consistent presence on the church calendar. Some churches offered them monthly; other churches offered them quarterly. But people knew when they were available and knew they were consistently offered.

- More times than not, the pastor either led the class or was a visible presence in the class. The presence of the pastor made a big statement to the priority of the class in the life of the church.

- Though there were a few exceptions, most of the new members' classes in the scrappy churches were three hours or less in length. They were typically offered on a Sunday in one block of time. I heard from many of the pastors how it was difficult to do multi-day classes. Absentees were common on some of the days of the multi-day sessions.

- Perhaps, most importantly, was *what* was communicated in these classes. First, the classes provided *information* on the church: doctrine, polity, staff, layout of facilities, denominational background (if any), and ministries and programs.

- Scrappy churches, however, made sure the classes communicated *information*, but they communicated *expectations* as well. "We make certain we let them know what is expected of them as a church member," Robin said. "We don't hesitate to talk about getting involved in community groups, being a faithful giver, and getting involved in a ministry. We have found that if we raise the bar of expectations, the commitment of the church member rises accordingly. We actually go over every chapter of your book *I Am a Church Member* to show them biblically what it means to be a part of the body of Christ."

It becomes easy to see how each of these four main emphases work together to close the back door. Like the Turnaround Cycle itself, Backdoor Closure is not as much a single point as it is a description of interworking parts. Some scrappy church pastors grasp these realities intuitively; for others it is learned behavior. It really doesn't matter. The key issue is a determined leader leading a determined congregation with actions that make a profound, if not eternal, difference.

That is why we call them scrappy churches.

The Turnaround Cycle and Scrappy Churches

We don't call the process the Turnaround Cycle without good reason. In each of the churches we studied, and all the leaders we interviewed, we heard clear and powerful stories of congregations that were once in decline, some even in steep decline, that are now growing as healthy churches.

At the risk of redundancy, we want to remind you that these stories were more than numerical turnarounds. For certain, we saw clear objective data that pointed to numerical reversals. But, as we interviewed leaders and church members, as we heard from people in the communities of these congregations, we saw transformation: transformation of attitudes, transformation of facilities, transformation of ministries, transformation of communities, and, for the glory of God, transformation of lives.

As we move to the final chapter, we will do more than report on other churches; we will talk about *your* church. It is my prayer that you will understand clearly and powerfully that the same God whose power is evident in these incredible turnaround stories desires for your church to experience that same transformation. Maybe God is calling your church right now to that path.

Maybe your congregation is about to become the next scrappy church.

CHAPTER 6

The Next Scrappy Church

THERE ARE A LOT OF DOOM-AND-GLOOM ATTITUDES ABOUT churches today. I know. I have been one of the most vocal about the state of our congregations.

On the one hand, I want us to face reality. I don't want us to keep our heads in the sand. The first step to losing weight is stepping on the scales and seeing the bad news. The first step to getting on the Turnaround Cycle is seeing the bad news.

It's simple. We don't change unless we see the need to change.

So, we face reality and what do we see? We see about seven of ten churches losing ground, declining, and frustrated. We see about 7,000 North American churches closing their doors each year. We see infighting, conflicts, and contentious business meetings. We see strained budgets, strained attitudes, and strained relationships.

And how about the pastors and other leaders in these churches? You probably know the answer to this question, because you experience it every week. Many of you know the pain of seeing fewer people gather for worship each week. Some of you are dealing with budgets that just can't be stretched far enough.

Most of you know the pain of criticisms, second-guessing, and "suggestions" about how you can improve your leadership.

You get it.

You don't need another pundit like me telling you that church leadership and church life can really stink. You've smelled that pungent odor for years.

You want to know there is hope. You want to know there is a place for your leadership and your church in the shadows of that big church where so many people seem to be walking the worn path. You want to know you are making a difference. You started well. You have tried to continue well. You want to finish well.

You know the rapid pace of change and the changing face of culture. But you want to know if you and your church can be biblically relevant in these tumultuous times. You are asking, at least to yourself, "Can I really make a difference?" Perhaps a few of you are ready to throw in the towel. Your pain has limits and your endurance has been tested too far. There has to be more to life and church leadership than this reality.

I get it.

If there is a single message I pray you will hear from this book, it is very simple.

There is hope.

How can I make such an audacious claim? How can I spit in the wind of congregational realities? I think you know the answer. By now, you have heard from churches that are counter-intuitive. They don't have the massive numbers. They don't have the state-of-the-art facilities. They aren't necessarily the buzz of the town, the latest cool church for a season.

They are scrappy churches.

And though they are at the early stages of becoming a movement, they are very real. They are making a difference. They are powerful. Let me be very clear. They are being used by God in ways that could become revolutionary. And yes, in case you are wondering, I am a bit excited about this movement.

I have analyzed these churches. I have heard from their leaders. And I have seen the paths they have taken. As we close this chapter and this book, I want to return to that path. And I want to take this route so you can remember and, above all, so you can have hope.

In summary, with a bit of review, what do the scrappy church leaders do?

They Love Their Church and Their Church Members

I remember my first church like it was yesterday. The church was in sad shape. Typical worship attendance was seven. You read the number correctly; I did not leave off the zero. The church had not seen a person become a follower of Christ in more than twenty-five years. The facilities stunk. I mean they literally stunk. It took me a few weeks to get used to the moldy, musty odor without getting nauseated.

It was really a lousy church. And I told them so. I chastised them. I preached to them with an unloving edge. They could see and feel my frustration, even anger. But they had been beaten up so long that they took the negativity from me. For them, it was the normal Christian life.

Of course, they responded with negativity toward me as well. After all, that is the role of church members, isn't it? They are to keep the pastor and staff in line. They are to make critical comments at the most inopportune times. In fact, a negative comment right before or after the sermon is normative.

Such was the relationship between my church members and me: sometimes pastoral, mostly adversarial.

If someone had asked me if I loved my church, I would have responded with a hearty "yes." But the reality is I loved the church I wanted them to be more than the church they were.

I'm glad Jesus didn't accept me on those terms.

The good news is that God convicted me during a time of prayer on Saturday night before the Sunday service. He showed me through His Word how I practiced conditional love. He showed me my harsh attitude toward the church members.

He broke me.

The church members would later tell me something was different about me the very next Sunday. They could not pinpoint the difference. One of them said I seemed happier and more loving.

God taught me to love my church as He loved me. Of course, I never got it perfectly, not even close. But I did learn to love the church I had rather than the church I wanted them to be. It's kind of like how Jesus loves us, isn't it?

Yes, the church did grow. Instead of a church of seven, we became a church of seventy. But far more important than the numerical metrics were the changed attitudes. And the biggest change was in me, the pastor. Frankly, I was the one who needed the most work.

I tell you that story because it was my own journey toward becoming a scrappy church leader. Now I have heard from hundreds of scrappy church leaders. Their stories are not identical, but they have commonalities. And one of the most often mentioned commonalities is their commitment to love their churches unconditionally.

Did you get that last word: *unconditionally*? They loved them despite their criticisms. They loved them despite their sporadic attendance. They loved them despite their quarrels and differences.

It seems like they loved them a bit like Jesus loves us.

"It was the turning point in my ministry," Aaron told us. "When I began to pray that God would give me the heart to love my church members unconditionally, my ministry was revolutionized. To be sure, it was not always easy. I still had some frustrating moments. But I voiced a prayer to God on a regular basis. He changed my heart and attitude. He changed my ministry. Instead of looking for the next church, I became content in the church He had given me."

They Love Their Community

Your church address is not an accident. God placed your church in your community for a reason. You are to love the community. You are to demonstrate that love by going to them, by ministering to them, and by showing the love of Christ to them.

The story of Michael is worth hearing. He has been pastor of a church in Nevada for eight years. Michael actually saw a progressive change in his attitude toward the community. In fact, he can identify the change in clearly marked stages.

"The first stage of my attitude toward the community was *apathy*," Michael shared. "I was frustrated so many community members either didn't attend church at all, or they went to the campus of a large multi-site church. If they didn't want anything to do with us, I sure wasn't interested in them."

Michael continued, "I really just confirmed the defeated attitudes of the church members when I came. They saw themselves as a holy huddle, and I got right in the middle of the huddle."

But the pastor had to make some pragmatic changes. The apathetic holy huddle was leading to decline. "I could read the handwriting on the wall," Michael said bluntly. "Our holy huddle was getting smaller. The budget was shrinking too. We had to reach more people, or we would be in trouble."

So, Michael began implementing programs and events to reach the community. "My heart for the community did not change," he admitted. "But I moved into a second stage I called *attractional*. I just wanted the community to come to us so we could sustain our ministry. It really was a selfish attitude. It didn't work well, either. People would come to our church for a certain event or program, but they wouldn't stick. I'm sure they sensed our less-than-genuine attitude," he admitted.

But it took a municipal election to begin the process of change in Michael's heart. "Jeremy was one of our young adult leaders at the church," Michael said, "and he decided to run for city council. He ran a great campaign and defeated the incumbent pretty handily."

Within a few months, Jeremy was getting his pastor involved in the community. He was showing how many good things were taking place. But he was also showing him the pain and challenges in many pockets of the community.

"Jeremy had a love for our community," Michael said. "It was contagious. I began to have a growing love for the community as well. Steadily, my attitude shifted. Instead of seeing people in the community as a means to grow our attendance and pay our bills, I saw them more and more as Jesus saw them. I began to love my community. I mean it. I began to absolutely love my community."

Michael did not throw out the attractional programs and events, but he led the church to do them with a love for the community. More church members caught the vision and the enthusiasm. "I really forgot about my angst about the campus church near us," Michael laughed. "I became so focused on loving the people in the community that I didn't have time to worry about the big church. I called this stage, my favorite part, the *incarnational* stage."

Scrappy church leaders love their community. And Michael's last statement is a reminder of something else scrappy church leaders do. They love other churches in the community.

They Love Other Churches in the Community

"We already have too many churches in our community."

"I can't believe they put a campus church so close to our church."

"That church will do anything to get people to attend there."

"If we had the money that church has, we could be a mega-church too."

"It's a shame how much money that church spends on marketing. They could be using it to feed the poor."

Have you ever heard any of those comments or similar comments? Have you ever heard animosity and/or jealousy expressed toward other churches? Have you ever wondered why some churches seem more like rivals than partners?

Scrappy churches take the higher road. They learn to love the churches in the community.

Though someone might point to a situation otherwise, I cannot recall ever seeing a community with too many churches. Indeed, the unchurched population of most communities is indicative we need more churches rather than fewer churches.

Scrappy church leaders get it. They see other churches as partners in ministry rather than competitors in business.

Logan said it well: "When I decided to partner with and love other churches in the community, it was like a big load lifted off me. I hadn't realized how much energy I had put forth toward being frustrated at other churches. It was so freeing to love the churches rather than loathe the churches."

Logan's church followed his leadership. They featured a church in the community every week as a focus of prayer. The congregation mentioned and prayed for a different church in each worship service. The prayer ministry team sent cards of prayer and thanksgiving to the staff and members of the featured church.

But the biggest change in attitude took place when Logan's church began to help other churches as mission projects. "Our members always thought we had to go out of town to do missions or to do a missions project. We added local churches as part of our missions effort, and it had a huge impact on our church," Logan told us.

The impetus for the missions project at a local church took place after a heavy storm. A church about four blocks away sustained some damage and debris from fallen limbs. "We had a team on site with chainsaws within an hour after the storm passed," Logan said with a beaming smile. "It was an incredible breakthrough for our church members. We really saw it as our mission to love and minister to other churches."

They Ate an Elephant

How do you eat an elephant? *One bite at a time.*

Scrappy church leaders get that reality. They understand that progress is often three steps forward and two steps backward. They often think in units of three to five years in order to see momentum change and progress made.

That is why most scrappy church leaders have the perspective of longer tenure. They see their relationship with the church as a relationship for the long haul. They understand there will be setbacks. But they persevere. They move forward. They know today's problems will be tomorrow's solutions.

It is not easy to eat an elephant. To add metaphor upon metaphor, the grass will seem greener in other churches. There will be temptations to leave for that greener grass. And there will be temptations to leave even if there is not a greener grass opportunity. There will be such moments of frustration that *any* opportunity will seem better than the present, even if it means unemployment.

Hear me well. I am not suggesting God will never call you from one church to the next. He has. He does. And He will. But I am suggesting that overall average pastoral tenure is much lower than it should be for effective ongoing leadership.

Scrappy church leaders are in it for the long haul. They accept incremental change and incremental progress. They don't bolt at the first few voices of criticism. They love the members unconditionally.

Scrappy church leaders eat an elephant.

They Lead an Outward Deluge

Let's return to the Turnaround Cycle for a moment. Once again let's see the simplified three main points of the cycle.

Review again the chapter on Outward Deluge. The two words are vital to understanding its import. First, *outward* means the church is constantly looking beyond itself. It is not obsessed with doing ministry and spending resources on only those who are presently in the church. In setting after setting, the members and the leaders are making themselves evaluate the outward efforts of their congregation.

The second word is *deluge*. Keep in mind the word means a constant and heavy flood. It is not something that comes for a season and is over. It is a steady and heavy outpouring. You must grasp this reality. Cultural Christianity is dead. Easy growth is over. Your church must be doing something outwardly on an ongoing basis.

Certainly, there will be times of special events and emphases. But your church must be scrappy. It must find a way to have ongoing outward efforts.

Scrappy church leaders point their congregations toward an outward focus. Regularly. Persistently. Enthusiastically.

Scrappy churches have an Outward Deluge.

They Prepare a Welcome Readiness

At the risk of redundancy, let me point you again to my book *Becoming a Welcoming Church*. The reason I am so excited about the book is the input I received from scrappy church leaders to write it. They told me repeatedly that one of the big steps toward getting their churches looking outwardly was helping members see through the eyes of guests.

"I was looking for some low-hanging fruit to change our perspective," Sarah told us. Sarah leads the entire outreach ministry of Shocco Life Church. The congregation of 140 had slowly become inwardly focused over a few years. Fortunately, the pastor saw the erosion and asked Sarah to help lead the church outwardly.

"The first thing I did was ask an unbeliever to visit our church," Sarah said with enthusiasm. "She completed a survey of her experience and shared it in our business meeting. Goodness gracious, it was eye-opening for all of us! We thought we were a friendly and caring church, but she said we were unfriendly, uncaring, and even rude at times."

Sarah paused and continued, "But I've got to give our people credit. Rather than get defensive and angry, they started seeking to change. They wanted Shocco Life Church to become a welcoming church. That was a tipping point for us. It led to us having a greater outward focus in many different ways. Eventually it led us to find ways to close the back door and retain the new people we were reaching."

What is fascinating about the story of Shocco Life Church is where they began on the Turnaround Cycle: Welcome Readiness. From that point they began to emphasize Outward Deluge and then Backdoor Closure. As with many of the scrappy churches, committing to one point on the Turnaround Cycle leads to getting healthier at other points.

They Focus on Backdoor Closure

The three points on the Turnaround Cycle are not mutually exclusive; they are complementary. As the church reaches more people and welcomes more people, they seek to retain those they have reached and welcomed.

Go back to the chapter on Backdoor Closure. See the emphasis scrappy churches have on small groups or Sunday school classes. See the priority they place on a membership class or some similar entry point. See how they communicate not only information about the church, but also expectations of those who are a part of the church. See how involvement in ministry is expected as a part of the rhythm of the church. See how the church raises the bar of expectations. People stay. People stick. They want to be a part of something that makes a difference.

Scrappy churches focus on Backdoor Closure.

They Believe God Is Not Done with Them or Their Churches

In Zechariah 4, the angel of the Lord appears to the prophet and priest, Zechariah. The angel has a message for Zerubbabel, the weak governor of Judah. At this point in Israel's history, she was not a nation but a province of Persia. Thus, Zerubbabel was a governor instead of a king.

The God-given task of Zerubbabel was clear: rebuild the house of God. After rebuilding the temple foundation for the first two years, construction came to a standstill for seventeen years. Yes, you read that right. Two years of building, then seventeen years of nothing.

Why did Zerubbabel stop? What led to his fear and/or apathy? For certain, there was opposition from outsiders who disrupted the building project (Ezra 4:4). But how did one opposing group have so much power? Why did the building of the house of God come to a standstill for almost two decades?

Why was there widespread fear? Was there pervasive discouragement? Was there a foreboding sense of apathy that was more dangerous than any opposing forces from the outside?

Can you imagine the conversations of those who passed the temple construction for seventeen years and saw nothing but a foundation? Did they murmur? Did they say, "That's a shame"? Did they say, "Somebody should do something about it?"

Or more likely, did they become so accustomed to the unbuilt house of God that they stopped noticing it? They walked around the temple foundation as if it were nothing more than a large rock to be avoided.

Then God spoke.

He spoke to Zechariah the prophet and priest rather than speaking directly to Zerubbabel. Maybe that was the path of God's protocol. Or maybe God just knew Zerubbabel did not have a listening ear, that his heart had grown cold with fear, doubts, and, then, apathy.

But God did speak. Read His words carefully In Zechariah 4:8–9: "Then the word of the LORD came to me: 'Zerubbabel's hands have laid the foundation of this house, and his hands will complete it. Then you will know that the LORD of Armies has sent me to you.'"

Did you get that?

Despite Zerubbabel's fears, despite his doubts, despite his weaknesses, and despite his years of apathy, he will complete the building of the house of God. And after the house of God is built, the world will know that God sent him to build it, that God was in it all.

Scrappy church leaders know God is not done with them. Scrappy church leaders know that as long as they have a breath to breathe, God wants them to build His church.

They don't have to be the largest church in town. They don't have to have the coolest facilities. Different servants of the living God are given different talents. The only option we don't have is to bury our talent, to do nothing with what God has given us.

You, church leader and church member, are on a mission field. That mission field is no less important than the distant mission fields. The mission field 9,000 miles away is no more or less important than the mission field nine blocks away.

Samaria and the end of the earth is important. And so is Jerusalem.

You have been called to your mission field for such a time as this. That field demands you use your talent. Use it. Invest it. Make a difference with it. But don't bury it.

God has called you to build His house. He has promised His hands will complete it.

Go, Therefore, and Make Disciples, Scrappy Churches

Scrappy.
Feisty.
Tenacious.
Determined.
Dogged.
Persistent.

That's how we started this book. But we must add a critical prepositional phrase. Scrappy churches are indeed feisty. They are tenacious. They are determined. They are dogged. And, yes, they are persistent. But they are all these things *in God's power.* That is really more than a prepositional phrase. It is an acknowledgment that we can do nothing without His power. And it is an affirmation that we can do all things in His power.

It is time to rid ourselves of powerlessness. Scrappy churches move mightily in God's power.

It is time to stop crying, "We don't have resources." Scrappy churches realize they have all the resources God has given them.

It is time to stop blaming others: the community, other churches, the denomination, and the culture. Scrappy churches know that God is greater than any obstacles or circumstances they would ever encounter.

It is time to move forward with a boldness that won't hinder us and a persistence that moves us on despite the critics, the naysayers, and the ones dying of terminal apathy.

It is time to embrace this one life God has given us, this one opportunity we have.

It is time to make disciples because God has promised He will be with us.

It is time.

It is time for scrappy churches to rise up and become a mighty movement in this land for this season.

And God has called you to lead it and join Him in it.

After all, that's what scrappy churches do.

SECRET GUEST SURVEY

CHURCH NAME

Thank you for taking time to be a secret church guest at our church. You are truly providing a helpful ministry to us. While we do not expect you to answer all of these questions in your report, we provide them as a general guide for you in this process.

If you do not have sufficient space, please add space electronically, or add pages if you are completing this report manually. If you have questions after reviewing this document, feel free to contact us at _____

A. Prior to going to the church, review the means to determine the location of the church and times for the church services:

1. Does the church have a website? If so, is it helpful? User-friendly?
    Does it provide the information you need to get to the church on time?

    _____

    _____

    _____

    _____

    _____

2. What conclusions do you reach about the church based on its website?

    _____

    _____

    _____

    _____

    _____

B. Having driven to the church and entered the parking lot, consider these questions:

1. Was it difficult to find the building? Would a person naturally drive by this building, or must you be intentionally going to this building to find it?

   _____
   _____

2. What are your thoughts as you view this church from the road? Based upon your first view of the buildings, what is your impression of the church?

   _____
   _____
   _____

3. Is there a church sign? If so, is it helpful?

   _____

4. Is guest parking available? If so, how is it marked? Are there signs directing you to guest parking?

   _____
   _____

5. Are there greeters in the parking lot?

   _____

6. Is the parking lot adequate? Convenient to the main entrance?

   _____
   _____
   _____

7. Is there a convenient auto passenger loading/unloading area? Is it covered for use in inclement weather?

   _____
   _____
   _____

8. Is it easy to locate the main entrance? Do you immediately know where to go to enter for church services?

   _____
   _____

C. As you enter the church, consider these questions:

1. As you enter, what are your first impressions of the entry foyer?
    Rate the following characteristics on a scale of 1 to 5:

UNINVITING   INVITING

(1)   (2)   (3)   (4)   (5)

Why?

COLD ATMOSPHERE   WARM ATMOSPHERE

(1)   (2)   (3)   (4)   (5)

Why?

CLUTTERED   TIDY

(1)   (2)   (3)   (4)   (5)

Why?

CONFUSING   STRAIGHTFORWARD

(1)   (2)   (3)   (4)   (5)

Why?

UNFRIENDLY   FRIENDLY

(1)   (2)   (3)   (4)   (5)

Why?

---

2. Is there adequate space in the foyer for people to talk and fellowship before and after worship services without blocking the main circulation path?

_____
_____
_____
_____

3. Is the circulation pattern clear?
   Do you know how to get to various areas of the building?

_____
_____
_____

4. Is there a clearly marked guest/welcome center?

_____
_____

5. Are there adequate signs to help you find your way?

_____
_____
_____

D. If you attend a small group (which is strongly our preference), respond to these questions:

1. Are there greeters who help you get to the appropriate classroom?

_____
_____
_____

2. What is your first reaction to the education areas?

_____
_____
_____

3. Do the classrooms appear large enough to make them usable for various age groups and teaching methods?

_____
_____

4. Are there room identification signs?

5. If you have children, is there a security/identification process in place to help identify your child/children?

6. How do you feel about leaving your children in the classrooms?
   (IMPORTANT: IF YOU HAVE ANY DISCOMFORT AT ALL, DO NOT LEAVE YOUR CHILDREN).

7. Do the classroom leaders secure needed information from you (e.g., name, address, allergies for children, your location in the building if needed in an emergency)?

8. Do preschool and children's rooms communicate a sense of security and warmth?

9. After attending a small group, rate the experience on the basis of:
   a. quality of the teaching

   b. friendliness of the group

   c. preparedness of the group — that is, were they ready to welcome and include a guest?

10. Would you attend a small group at this church again?

E. In the worship center, consider these questions:

1. What are your first feelings and thoughts as you enter? Why?

_____

_____

_____

_____

_____

2. Does this space feel welcoming? Why?

_____

_____

_____

_____

_____

_____

3. Does the worship space say anything to you about this congregation and its priorities?

_____

_____

_____

_____

_____

_____

4. Is there appropriate quality in materials and craftsmanship? Does anything look cheap, too showy, out of place?

_____

_____

_____

_____

_____

_____

_____

5. Rate the worship space on the following characteristics, on a scale of 1 to 5:

POOR ACOUSTICS   EXCELLENT ACOUSTICS

(1)   (2)   (3)   (4)   (5)

Why? _____

NOT COMFORTABLE   VERY COMFORTABLE

(1)   (2)   (3)   (4)   (5)

Why? _____

UNFRIENDLY   FRIENDLY

(1)   (2)   (3)   (4)   (5)

Why? _____

VERY UNATTRACTIVE   VERY ATTRACTIVE

(1)   (2)   (3)   (4)   (5)

Why? _____

ORDINARY   CREATIVE
ARCHITECTURE   ARCHITECTURE

(1)   (2)   (3)   (4)   (5)

Why? _____

COLD,   WARM
INTIMIDATING   FRIENDLY SPACE

(1)   (2)   (3)   (4)   (5)

Why? _____

6. As a guest, did you feel uncomfortable in any way? Affirmed in any way?

_____

_____

7. If the church provided you any documents (e.g., bulletin, worship guide, etc.), are the documents high quality? Did they facilitate worship for you in any way?

_____

_____

8. Rate the overall experience on the basis of:
   a. quality of the music

   _____

   b. style of the music

   _____

   c. friendliness of the congregation

   _____

   d. quality of the preaching

   _____

   _____

   e. clarity in instruction — did you know and understand what the church expected participants to do at all points in the service?

   _____

   _____

   f. use of PowerPoint or other media to make announcements, outline sermon, etc.

   _____

   _____

9. What one improvement would you suggest regarding the worship service?

   _____

   _____

   _____

10. Would you return to this church to worship with this congregation?

   _____

   _____

   _____

F. Summary

1. What are your overall impressions of this church based on this visit?

_____

_____

_____

_____

_____

_____

_____

_____

_____

_____

2. Would you return to visit this church? Why or why not?

_____

_____

_____

_____

_____

_____

_____

_____

_____

_____

Your goal is to provide us information that simply tells your experience in this church.
Be honest and clear.
Thank you again for your willingness to assist

_____

CHURCH NAME

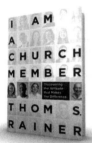

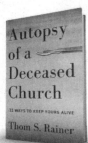
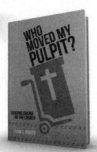